Be Encouraged!

Letters That Will Build You Up in a Tear You Down World

John D. Gillespie

Myrrh Books,
Overland Park, Kansas

Be Encouraged!

Letters That Will Build You Up in a Tear You Down World

John D. Gillespie

Myrrh Books, Overland Park, Kansas, USA
ISBN -ISBN-13: 978-1534853591
ISBN-10: 1534853596

Be Encouraged!

Welcome

Dear Friends,

In a sense I have written this little book to myself. Why? I need *encouragement*! I struggle with discouragement; I am too easily knocked off course. So, in some ways this is an exercise in necessary self-indulgence. I need to remind myself often ... daily ... hourly ... moment by moment ... of the goodness of the Lord.

The Lord Jesus is endlessly encouraging. Even in His warnings there are encouragements to press on and to not lose heart. He wants to build us up, for discouraged disciples are not only of lesser use to His Gospel cause, but He loves us – each and every one of us – and therefore wants us to be *encouraged* in Him.

Many of these letters were first written to my dear congregation at Grace Community Church in Cornwall. They flowed from a pastor's heart for his people. They have been polished up just a bit for this book, but you will still find a rough edge or two (I don't mind, if you don't).

While I am in no way pretending that this little book will go down in Christian history as a great work, I do think that there are a few gems to brighten your walk with Jesus within its pages. It does not merit being on a shelf next to Tozer or Lewis. Keep it in your car or back-pack, by your bed or in the bath. Give it to a friend.

So, please take these little letters and let them encourage you in Jesus Christ. I know that He wants you built up in Him, that you may be able to enjoy Him as your Saviour, and be a useful vessel of His grace in this desperate world. Please take them as from my heart to yours, for if we could sit together I know that we would waste little time before we were building one another up in Jesus. That is just what Christ's Followers inevitably do.

It is a *Joy* to share words of encouragement with you.

John Gillespie,

May 2016, London Heathrow Central Bus Station (missed my bus by 10 minutes)

P.S. Having lived most of my formative years in the USA and most of my adult years to date in England, and being a citizen of both, I tend to jumble UK/USA spelling, phraseology, and word use. Apologies to purists in either world! Please do not let this colour (color?) your enjoyment of this little book.

Be Encouraged!

Faith Works

By faith Moses, when he had grown up, refused to be known as the son of Pharaoh's daughter. He chose to be ill-treated along with the people of God rather than to enjoy the pleasures of sin for a short time. He regarded disgrace for the sake of Christ as of greater value than the treasures of Egypt, because he was looking ahead to his reward. By faith he left Egypt, not fearing the king's anger; he persevered because he saw Him who is invisible. By faith he kept the Passover, and the sprinkling of blood, so that the destroyer of the firstborn would not touch the firstborn of Israel.
Hebrews 11:24-29

Dear People of Faith,

Take some time and read the passage above from Hebrews Chapter Eleven. Don't rush over it. ... Meditate on it, chew on it, see how much "goodness" you can get out of it.

All right, now have you really taken some time over that amazing paragraph? Well, let's take some more time. It is an action paragraph if ever there was one. Go back, and *count up* how many "things" Moses did in that paragraph. Go ahead ...

I count at least eight positive things he did, and one very important thing that he did not do ... all "by faith". That is stated three times in the passage.

Before we look at Moses' actions, let's just remind ourselves that, according to the Book of Hebrews, "Faith" always deals with two things: 1) The Future 2) The Invisible:

Now faith is being sure of what we hope for [The Future], and certain of what we do not see [The Invisible].
(Hebrews 11:1)

7

So, just what was Moses able to "do" by this faith in the Unseen God who holds the Future?

(I think this is really exciting and inspiring!)

1) He *Refused* something: He could have had an easy life of luxury in Pharaoh's family, but he was gripped by a vision of a future reward and an invisible Christ! The present and what was seen lost their power over him!

2) He *Chose* something: Ill treatment along with God's despised people rather than short-term gratification. He made a *decision* to forego present, sinful pleasure, because he had a certain hope of a future Joy.

3) He *Regarded* something: Disgrace for Christ was more valuable than earthly treasure. Faith assured and convinced him of a future reward of greater worth than all the treasures of Egypt.

How powerful, this faith!

Let's carry on ...

4) He *looked ahead* to something: "His reward." Remember, faith deals with the future and can wait; unbelief deals with the present and must "have it all" now. There is a holy reward ahead for every child of faith. Believe it.

5) He *left* something: Namely, Egypt. That is, all he knew, all his comforts, all his earthly luxury and security. His heart was fixed upon something future and unseen. He could no longer be bribed by the moment. He became a pilgrim and a sojourner in this life.

6) He *did not fear* someone (This is the important thing that he did *not* do because of faith): The King's anger lost its grip on his soul. Faith in the Invisible God of Tomorrow delivered him from fear in the visible king of the day. Think about that! Glory!

7) He *persevered in* something: He did not give up on the call of God upon his life when things got tough, for the simple, but profound reason that the eyes of his soul beheld what only Faith can see. Seeing God Himself as his Prize gave him encouragement for the long road ahead.

8) He *Saw* something: Or rather, Someone, invisible to the natural eye. Someone no telescope or microscope can reveal. Someone so Beautiful and Terrible (I am using the word in the old-fashioned way), that all things visible took on their proper perspective.

9) He *kept* something: The Sprinkling of Blood. It made no scientific sense. It was not politically correct. But the Invisible One had told him to do it, so he did it ... and he and all Israel were delivered from God's wrath because of it.

FAITH! Not vague, undefined, wispy notions, but real confidence in the Invisible God who holds Tomorrow... the God who holds Time in His hands, and who sent His Son to be an atoning sacrifice for our sins. Faith is powerful and life-changing. It produces action. It rouses the soul. It emboldens the will. It realigns the priorities. It empowers the weary. It redefines the good life.

Real Faith sets us to work. It causes us to make great decisions, living *in the now* in the light of *Eternity.* It causes us to treasure Jesus Christ Himself above all, and sets us free to Live.

And without it, it is:

... impossible to please God (Hebrews 11:6).

May the Lord Jesus Himself give us Grace to "look ahead to our reward," and to see "Him who is Invisible."

Accept no substitutes.

Your Fellow Sojourner.

9

Be Encouraged!

There are Blessings for the Battles

Consecrate yourselves, for tomorrow the Lord will do amazing things among you.
Joshua 3:5

Dear Friend in Christ,

Do you ever find yourself reading your Bible when suddenly a verse, one which you have read many times before, comes to life before you and speaks to you as though you have never even seen it before?

Well, this happened to me recently while I was having my early morning quiet time. I was sitting in my father's chair at his home in Kansas City reading the book of Joshua, when the following verse jumped up and grabbed me:

"Consecrate yourselves, for tomorrow the Lord will do amazing things among you."

Now, you need to believe me when I tell you that I actually believe that God *speaks* to me (and to all who are ready to listen) through the Bible. My quiet times with God are life and breath to me because I meet with Him through His Word ... He speaks to my heart and into my life situation almost everyday.

He spoke to me in the verse above, and I am pleased to share with you what He shared with me.

First, let's remember the background:

Israel had been wandering for forty years in the wilderness, God forbidding them to enter the Promised Land due to their sin of unbelief. Moses, their leader through those years of disobedience was now dead and buried, and Joshua had succeeded him as the leader of God's Israel. It was Joshua who was to lead Israel over the Jordan to take possession of the land He had promised to them.

What plans God had for them! He was to lead them in victory over their enemies and establish them as His prized people, as a testimony to all the world of His grace and power. He was about to fulfill in them the promises he had made centuries before to Abraham. He was about to prove Himself to be their Covenant-Keeping Faithful God in giving them their long-promised inheritance. He was ready to "do wondrous things" among them.

But God's readiness and willingness led to a call for consecration among God's people. This was what grabbed my heart on that early morning in Kansas City. "Consecrate yourselves ... for tomorrow I will do wondrous things among you." To consecrate yourself means

*To set yourself apart from all that is unholy.

*To repent of any sin that may be found in you.

*To get serious about God again.

*To open up your heart to the Lord in a new way.

God was not going to take a half-hearted, worldly people into the Promised Land. Such a people would never stand up to the battles and challenges involved in taking that land for the Lord. More so, a worldly, carnal Israel would make a mess of God's abundant goodness, receiving the blessings, while forgetting the Lord.

An unconsecrated people are unfit both for the battles and the blessings God has in store for them.

Likewise, what was true for ancient Israel is true for me today.

*Does God want to bless me? *YES*

*Does God want to lead me to victory in battle? *YES*

*Does God have great plans for me as His son? *YES*

*Does God have glorious purposes for me? *YES*

Can God use me as fully as He desires if I am half-converted, worldly, selfish and essentially no different from the world around me?

NO!

My private life matters. My relationships matter. What I think about matters. How I spend my money matters. What I say matters. My habits and hobbies matter.

Every aspect of my life matters and needs to be consecrated - set apart - for God's greater Glory. Half-heartedness is an offence to our Gracious God and stifles His Glorious Purposes for us.

God's word to Israel so long ago is a word for us today. Now is the time for me to rid myself of all that is not holy, and to open my heart yet more to the Lord, for His Heart is to do "wondrous things" in my life and circumstances. God has battles for me to fight ... and win, and blessings for me to receive with rejoicing.

God wants and wills "to do wondrous things among us," but the key is in our hands ... and hearts: "Consecrate yourselves." Let us not be afraid of Holiness of Heart and Life. Allow me to get "up close and personal" for just a moment or two: What will "consecrating yourself" *look like* in *your* life?

*What choices will you have to make?

*What repentances might you have to offer?

*What relationships may need to be mended?

*What shape will "dying to self" take in your life?

Don't allow yourself to dodge these questions. Your ability to fight and win the battles God has for you, to scale the mountains He has for you, and to inherit the blessings He has for you, depends upon your ardent willingness to "consecrate yourself" to Him.

But, the challenge cannot rest with me, or with you, as individuals. The challenge from Joshua 3:5 was for Israel *as a people.* God is calling *us*, not just me, not just you, but *US*, as a company of believers, a body of believers, to "consecrate ourselves" ... as individuals *who belong to* each other. How we each rise to this will have an effect upon the whole. As a church God has battles for *us* to fight and win for the Gospel, and abundant blessings for *us* to inherit.

Consecrating myself is about something bigger than my battles, and my blessings. In the end it is about the welfare of the People of God, and the advancement of the cause of Christ on Earth ... even for generations to come.

Beloved, God wants and wills to "do wondrous things among us." May we, each one, and as a whole "Consecrate ourselves" in every way to Him, that we may be in the place to fight and win battles and receive and rejoice in blessings.

Yours, But for a Higher Purpose.

Be Encouraged!

Wasting Your Life For Jesus is Never a Waste!

While Jesus was in Bethany in the home of a man known as Simon the Leper, a woman came with an alabaster jar of very expensive perfume, which she poured on his head as he was reclining at the table. When the disciples saw this, they were indignant. "Why this waste?" they asked. "This perfume could have been sold at a high price and the money given to the poor."
Matthew 26:6-8

Dear Saints,

Contemplate the above scene with me. It is rich with meaning for those of us who dare to call ourselves disciples of Jesus Christ.

Imagine yourself for a moment as Simon, the Leper whom Christ had healed. In gratitude you are happy to have a dinner party for Jesus Christ! Everything *must* be perfect as you make preparations for this most important evening: the food, the entertainment, the music, the table carefully set.

As Jesus and the other guests arrive, you, in keeping with social custom of the day, offer each a drop of perfume for his tired feet (don't try that today!). Jesus and the others receive it with thanks and come to recline at your table.

You're nervous, expectant ... excited ...

Then, suddenly, unexpectedly, unconventionally, your party is ... Crashed!

(Now, switch places and imagine yourself as this gate-crashing woman.)

You know the custom: women are to stay outside of the dining room at a formal party ... But this is your chance!

You have heard about a prostitute who poured perfume on Jesus' feet in the early days of his ministry, wiping them with her hair (Luke 7:36ff) "Wow," you've thought: "If ever I have the chance to bless Him in such a manner, I am going for it."

Your heart is beating a mile a minute as you approach the house, move past the porch and through the opened door, beyond the foyer and courageously, into the presence of the dining men.

Jaws drop.

Eating stops.

Chatter ceases.

And then ... GASPS of shock and disgust as (according to Mark's Gospel), you *break* a vial of *most expensive* perfume and proceed to pour *the entire thing* upon the head of your beloved Jesus.

While Simon and the others are choking on their dinner, Jesus Christ is smiling, deep in enjoyment. You have broken convention: Not a drop on the feet, but a whole bottle on the head.

You have done what you can, while you can, with what you have to give.

The others, *even the disciples*, call this extravagance "waste." But you know that this is ...

WORSHIP.

Jesus knows it too.

This is Worship in the deepest and truest sense, perhaps the best example of worship in the whole of sacred Scripture. It goes beyond what is culturally acceptable and is a true expression of a redeemed heart toward its Redeemer. It regards not the opinions of lukewarm onlookers. It listens not to the rebukes of the culturally religious. It beholds only Christ, its object, and is blessed because *He* is blessed: "She has done a beautiful thing to me." (v.10)

Now, no more imagination: Be yourself now. Let's *learn* from this remarkable scene and *apply* it to our lives today.

1) The worshipping life which blesses Jesus Christ may be misunderstood by others.

2) The worshipping life which blesses Jesus Christ may shatter cultural boundaries.

3) The worshipping life which blesses Jesus Christ gives what it can, when it can.

4) The worshipping life which blesses Jesus Christ is extravagant, not calculating.

5) The worshipping life which blesses Jesus Christ becomes an unstoppable fragrance.

6) The worshipping life which blesses Jesus Christ will leave a lasting legacy of faith.

The Holy Spirit did not feel it worthwhile to tell us what Simon made for dinner, what others wore, what music was being played. What impresses men often means little to God. What the Holy Spirit wanted to be sure was remembered was this beautiful act of worship.

Sometimes the conventional just won't do.

May our lives learn from this woman. May our hearts long to bless our Redeemer, going beyond the expected to the extravagant. May we not be afraid to "waste" ourselves on Christ, knowing that in so doing, our very existence will become a fragrance to all, a witness to our culture that there is a Saviour whose name is Jesus Christ.

Yours, and Willing to be Wasted for His Name's Sake.

Be Encouraged!

With Jesus the Victim Becomes the Victor

As for you, you were dead in your transgressions and sins, in which you used to live when you followed the ways of this world and the ruler of the kingdom of the air, the spirit who is at work in those who are disobedient. All of us lived among them at one time gratifying the cravings of our sinful nature and following its desires and thoughts. Like the rest we were by nature objects of wrath.

Ephesians 2:1-3

Dear Fellow Victor in Jesus,

In 1944, Japanese soldier Lt. Hiroo Onoda was sent by his commanding officer to the remote Philippine island of Lubang to conduct guerilla warfare and spy upon his Allied enemies.

He surrendered thirty years later, in 1974.

He refused to believe that the war had ended.

As a teenager, I remember seeing the event on the news.

He had spent twenty-nine years fighting a war that had already been decided, battling on even though he had already been defeated. During those years he lived on the run, in hiding, on the lookout. He and the small troop of soldiers who held out with him (all of whom had died by 1974) had killed more than 30 Filipinos, believing themselves to be still in a state of hostility, convinced that victory would be theirs.

Onoda had had his chances. The Allies leafleted the island from the air telling of their victory and of the end of hostilities. He found the leaflets, but refused to believe that Japan could ever lose the war.

Island peoples, aware of his shadowy existence, left newspapers telling of peace where he could find them, but in his growing paranoia, he believed such news to be a hoax, or worse, a trap.

So he went on, polishing his rifle, living rough, keeping watch, and killing ... all for no purpose.

Finally, in 1974, his aged commanding officer, hearing of his existence, traveled himself to Lubang, found him, and gave him the now old news: He had been defeated long ago. ... It was time now to lay down the arms, and face the facts!

Can you imagine how he felt when he discovered the folly of his ways? We need not imagine. We have his words:

> "Suddenly a storm raged inside of me ...
> Everything went black ...
> I felt like a fool ..."*

Now the Onoda misadventure is pregnant with applications, but I want simply to draw out one, and then drive home a point.

I want you to imagine with me that our brave but blundering warrior is a picture of us as individuals ... at least of a part of us. I am referring to what theologians call the "sinful nature" or "the old man." Do you know that the "natural," once-born human being is actually *controlled by* a nature that is at war with God and refuses to surrender? As unpalatable as that might sound, it is what the Bible teaches. Hear the Apostle Paul on this:

> *As for you, you were dead in your transgressions*
> *and sins, in which you used to live when you*
> *followed the ways of this world and the ruler of the*
> *kingdom of the air, the spirit who is at work in*
> *those who are disobedient. All of us lived among*
> *them at one time gratifying the cravings of our*

---

* About.com: *The War is Over...Please come Out,* by Jennifer Rosenberg

sinful nature and following its desires and
thoughts. Like the rest we were by nature objects
of wrath. (Ephesians 2:1-3)

Now this sinful nature "naturally" has dominion over every one of us ... even over every baby born on this planet (just watch a crèche for a few minutes). The very guilt and pollution of Adam has been passed on to us, so that we now sin by nature and by choice. This is what theologians call the "Doctrine of Original Sin." Don't like that? Hear King David on this:

> *Surely I was sinful at birth,*
> *Sinful from the time my mother conceived me*
> ...(Psalm 51:5)

Now hear some Good News - good for your soul, but bad for your "sinful nature." Your "sinful nature" has been soundly defeated through the death of Jesus Christ on the Cross! A decisive victory has been secured over Satan and sin through the death and resurrection of Jesus Christ. Don't believe me? Well then, believe the Bible:

> *I [the "old man"] have been crucified with*
> *Christ, and I [the "old man"] no longer live, but*
> *Christ lives in me ...* (Galatians 2:20)

> *For we know that our old self [the old man]*
> *was crucified with him so that the body ruled by*
> *sin might be done away with, that we should no*
> *longer be slaves to sin.* (Romans 6:6)

We have moved Kingdoms, been given new natures, and have been adopted out of Adam's family (yes, the whole human race is naturally, literally "The Adam's Family"), and into Christ's.

Everything is New For the Believer:

Therefore, if anyone is in Christ, the new creation has come: The old
has gone, the new is here! (2 Corinthians 5:17)

19

But …

… There is a good chance that your sinful nature has not gotten the message.

And …

… As long as you give "him" the least bit of encouragement to fight on, he will. He will creep around, living in the shadowy areas of your life, hiding here and there, taking any and every opportunity to inflict damage and havoc, refusing to believe that he will ever be defeated.

What needs to happen to your "sinful flesh" is the same thing that needed to happen to Onoda. Somebody, namely *you*, needs to inform him, in no uncertain terms, that he has been defeated at Calvary, and he has *no chance of winning*. The Bible says so:

> *… count yourselves dead to sin but alive to God in Christ Jesus.* (Romans 6:11)

> *Sin shall not be your master, because you are not under the law, but under grace …* (Romans 6:14)

> *We were therefore buried with him through baptism into death, in order that, just as Christ was raised from the dead through the glory of the Father, we too may live a new life …* (Romans 6:4)

> *If any one is in Christ, he is a New Creation. The old has gone, the new has come …* (2 Corinthians 5:17)

> *So I say, live by the Spirit, and you will not gratify the desires of the sinful nature …* (Galatians 5:16)

We need to be tough on him, and give him no space for negotiations.

Look, the make-up of a human is very complex, and our sinful nature does not make figuring us out any easier. But the bottom line is that the Believer has a *new* nature, and the old nature needs to be told so… as often as necessary, until it gets the message ("crucifying the sinful nature" is a biblical way of saying the same thing). Could it be that a lot of us are living under the influence of an old foe that needs to be confronted with the FACT of Christ's victory, disarmed, and marched off in chains? Sin's *penalty* was paid for on Calvary's Cross, and sin's *power* was broken on that very same Cross!

Jesus Christ has come to set us free. Jesus said:

… if the Son sets you free, you will be free indeed. (John 8:36)

Is your "old man" still "at large," refusing to believe that he has been defeated on the Cross, holding you in bondage to sin, fear, and defeat? Tell him in no uncertain terms that *he* is finished and that *you* are now a New Creature, in Christ, created to do good works, pleasing to God, with a new heart and a new life, called "holy" by God Himself, uniquely *His*,

Yours, A Victor, and Not a Victim Anymore!

Be Encouraged!

The Marvel of Motherhood

Her children arise and call her blessed;
her husband also, and he praises her:
"Many women do noble things,
but you surpass them all."
Charm is deceptive, and beauty is fleeting; but a
woman who fears the Lord is to be praised.
Honor her for all that her hands have done, and let her
works bring her praise at the city gate.
Proverbs 31: 28-31

Brothers and Sisters,

I want to take just a few moments of your time to champion the sacred calling of motherhood.

What can be more important than the nurturing ministry of a mother? Yet ...

What calling is today more maligned and disregarded as "menial" than that of a mother?

Take just a moment and think about *your* mother. Perhaps she is still alive, perhaps long dead. This Mothering Sunday marks my first since my own mother's promotion to glory just three months ago. Don't be afraid to cry as you remember

-the smell of baked bread upon her apron,

-the sound of her bustling about in the kitchen,

-that look of wisdom in her smile, how her eyes could see right through you, and yet understand at the same time,

-the touches of artistry left all about your childhood home by her deft hand,

-the tears while nursing your skinned knee.

Whoever could replace a *Mother*? Why, it would take a small army of workers and a small fortune of finance to make up for the tireless labours of one selfless mother ... And they still would come up short, for a consecrated mother is a:

Nutritionist, Psychiatrist

Chauffer, Paramedic

Economist, Teacher

Bookkeeper, Diplomat

Beautician, Coach

Seamstress, Mechanic

Plumber, Jailer

Gardener, Theologian

She is on call 24/7, 365 days a year, and on top of that she needs to look beautiful for her husband (who, if he knows what is good for him, will value her above rubies, and make sure that she knows it!).

Who *sacrifices* like a mother? Who *serves* like a mother? Who *sees* like a mother? Who *suffers* like a mother?

Not all women are called to be married, and not all married women are called to be mothers. But, every one of us has, or has had, a mother! Where would we be without our mothers? For countless centuries strong cultures have been built upon the tender, strong love of mothers. It has been left to *our* generation to demean the sacred calling and tell our mothers that society can get along fine without their skillful dedication; that a woman's "personal fulfillment" is more important than a mother's sacrifice; that our government can nurture as well as, or perhaps better than, our mothers.

We fail to value and honour our mothers to our own peril.

Let's give "three cheers" for motherhood (we better, because our fool-hearty culture won't).

Let's value the "keeper of the home." Does your mother *know*, from your own lips, how dearly you value her?

Husband, does your wife *know* that you value her and her homemaking above all your possessions?

But, above all else, the *Christian* mother contributes to the Kingdom of God by nurturing and sending forth happy followers of Jesus Christ into a dark and needy world.

*Where would England be without Susannah, the Godly mother of the Wesleys?

*Where would the Church in China be today without the faithful prayers of Hudson Taylor's mother for her wayward son?

*Where would the Western mind be today without the steadfastness of the Godly Monica, praying mother of Augustine, the rebel turned Follower, who was to become perhaps the greatest Christian thinker of all time?

And such stories can be multiplied millions of times in the countless biographies of heroic mothers known only to God.

Can there be a more powerful weapon for Good than a Godly, praying *Mother*?

Our Lord Jesus hallowed Motherhood when He tabernacled in the womb of the young Mary. From the cross, He gave His beloved John charge to care for her, His dear mother. So may we too value our mothers, and the sacred calling of Motherhood, with grateful hearts.

Yours, forever grateful for my godly Mother.

Be Encouraged!

There is an Inexhaustible Source of Joy

... for the Joy of the Lord is Your Strength.
Nehemiah 8:10

Dear Church Family,

I want to let you in on my personal battle for Joy, and share with you one of my most precious discoveries. I am sure that I am not the only one who has found Joy to be often elusive; or perhaps not the only one who has often battled with a melancholy spirit.

Of two things we can be certain:

1) Jesus wants us Joyful.

2) Satan does not.

I could marshal countless Scriptures to prove the above two truths, but one will be sufficient for it falls from the lips of the Lord Jesus Himself:

The thief [you know who that is] *comes only to steal and kill and destroy. I have come that they* [that's us!] *may have life and have it to the full.* (John 10:10)

Now, true Joy goes deeper than happiness, and is not dependent upon shallow earthly origins. The verse at the top of this letter takes us right to the source of true Joy. This discovery has become *my* personal source of Joy. The verse establishes Joy in the very nature of God, and then makes the life-transforming link between *His* Joy and *our* well-being. Walk with me up the mount of God and refresh your soul with me in this Eternal Source of all Joy: God Himself.

Okay, here is the key to my discovery: God, the Eternal Triune Father, Son, and Holy Spirit **is in His very nature a Community of Joy.**

He likes being God. He has never been depressed. Within the relationship that is the Trinity there has never been an argument. Go to the spiritual heart of the Universe and there you will find our Triune God, *full of Joy*.

Now, just take some time and *think* about this. Let it wash over your Joy-parched soul. Let the Joy of the Lord slake *your* thirst for deep, deep Fullness. Our Joy is founded in the very nature of God. It is not originated, it *dare not be,* in anything less than the way that God actually *is.*

Allow a human analogy: As the head of my family, my mood sets the tone of the entire household. I am prone to moodiness (God is not). If I am in a sour mood, the kids are sad, my wife is affected, the entire household feels it. If I am glad, my home is glad. If my emotions are under peaceful control, my house is generally at peace. It is as simple and profound as that.

Now, our God is Joyful within Himself. Surely, God experiences the entire range of emotions as He interacts with His Creation. But beneath it all is the Joy that Eternally resides in the very heart of the Trinity. *His* Joy should affect *His* family, right down to you and me. If God is not freaking out, then I don't need to either. *His* mood needs to be the source, the determiner, of *my* mood.

This truth needs to be pondered. We have become too emotionally fragile. We are not resourcing ourselves in our changeless God, but in transient things. For years I have been at the mercy of my moods, a victim of the winds that blow about me (and blow me about). God has really been challenging me of late to deal with this ... impressing upon my heart that it is actually a sign of spiritual immaturity to allow myself to be affected by everything but Himself. To put it bluntly, if He is Joyful, I should be Joyful. It just may be a sinful, unbelieving heart which allows me to wallow in joyless melancholy when I am called to believe for, and battle for, Joy.

So, I have begun to battle instead of wallow, strengthening my spirit with Bible Truths. Among the most helpful Bible passages to me are Psalm 90:14; John 10:10; Psalm 1:1-3; John 17:13.

Boy! Do I have a long way to go, but having *seen* the truth that Joy resides at the relational centre of our Triune God, and that His Joy is available for my strengthening, a revolution has begun in my soul!

I hope that this is speaking to some hearts which, like mine, to one degree or another, have known unexplainable dark days. But just in case you need yet a bit more encouragement to believe that the Lord would like *His* Joy to be in *you,* let me leave you with the very words of our Lord Jesus. Take them, believe them, refuse to accept any less than what he is offering you:

As the Father has loved me, so have I loved you ... I have told you this so that my joy may be in you, and that your joy may be complete.
(John 15:9,11)

May the Joy that exists in the very nature of our God become for us an inexhaustible fount of fullness.

Yours in Grace, Peace and *Joy.*

Be Encouraged!

Jesus is Your Righteousness

Surely he hath borne our griefs, and carried our sorrows: yet we did esteem him stricken, smitten of God, and afflicted. But he was wounded for our transgressions, he was bruised for our iniquities: the chastisement of our peace was upon him; and with his stripes we are healed. All we like sheep have gone astray; we have turned every one to his own way; and the Lord hath laid on him the iniquity of us all.
Isaiah 53:4-6 KJV

Beloved of God,

There is a Truth upon which the entire Christian church stands or falls, and a Truth upon which we as Believers can live in freedom, joy and confidence. Here is the very centre of our Faith. Here is true health for our souls and nourishment for our lives.

Here is the doctrine of Justification by Grace, through Faith.

Now, don't, please don't, be put off in any way by the theological term, *Justification*. Rather, learn the meaning of the word and the power of the Truth embodied in it ... For *it has life-changing power*.

Justification is a change - a legal change - in a sinner's standing before our Holy God *because of the work that Jesus Christ accomplished for him on the cross*. Let's feast upon the Truth of what this means for us as Believers:

1) Our greatest and gravest need is for the sin problem in our lives to be somehow resolved before a sin-hating, offended God.

2) Our sin-problem has been dealt with through the Blood of Jesus Christ. Romans 4:5 tells us that God "justifies the wicked."

29

Romans 5:9 tells us that we have been "justified by His [Jesus'] blood." So, we are looking here not at something *we do for God*, but rather at something *God has done for us*.

3) Justification means *"to declare righteous."* It is *objective* (outside of me) rather than *subjective* (inside of me). It is, if I can be so bold, *a change in God's mind about me* because of the death of Jesus Christ for my sins. Where on my own I stand rightly condemned before God because of my sins, I now stand justified before God, that is declared righteous, because of Christ's death in my place.

4) You cannot be "more" or "less" Justified. It is like being married: You either are or are not! The Bible declares that "there is now *no condemnation* to them that are in Christ Jesus" (Romans 8:1). Satan, the enemy of your soul *does not want you to grasp this Truth!*

5) Justification is more than pardon. In pardon, one is guilty, but let off, released. Justification declares one righteous before a Holy Judge and therefore *welcomed* into God's family. Pardon says: "You don't deserve to go, but you may. Be on your way." Justification says: "I no longer have a case against you; you may come!" Our sins have been conclusively dealt with by Jesus Christ, and we are therefore warmly welcomed into fellowship with the Father.

6) Justification is not only the removal of guilt, it is also the crediting of righteousness. It is not just a "zero balance" but the gift of the very righteousness of Jesus Christ being given to the Believer! Romans 4:6 says that God "credits righteousness" to the believer "apart from works." Imagine! The righteousness of Jesus Christ given as a gift to the unrighteous! "God made Him who knew no sin to be sin on our behalf that in Him we might become the righteousness of God." (2 Corinthians 5:21)

7) Justification is Once for All. The Bible says that the Blood of Jesus perfects us "for all time" (see Hebrews 10:1-4); "having been justified by faith, we have peace with God" (Romans 5:1). This means that we do not lose our salvation every time we sin. We may lose our joy, we may spoil our testimony and need to undergo the chastisement of God, but he now treats us as "new creatures in Christ" (2 Cor 5:17)

8) We receive Justification through faith alone. Not faith in faith, but faith in Jesus Christ, and specifically in His atoning death and victorious resurrection. The Bible affirms "Believe in the Lord Jesus Christ and you shall be saved." (Acts 16:31) Paul speaks of being "found in him, not having a righteousness of my own that comes through the law, but that which is through faith in Christ - the righteousness that comes from God and is by faith." (Philippians 3:9)

Now, dear fellow believer, I encourage you to plant yourself in this rich Truth - that you may be secure in the Gospel even as you grow in grace and seek after holiness of heart and life. Contemplate this great Truth. Strengthen yourself with it. There is *no other anchor for the soul*. It will keep you through good and bad, success and failure, health and illness, and hold you fast when death's storm beats upon you. It is your sure and only hope as you face a day when you shall appear before the judgment seat of Christ. Justification by faith alone will provide the platform from which you can battle temptations, face trials, and overcome the enemy. It will give you a launch pad for missions, and a refuge when you crash and burn.

It is the only hope for the human soul.

> Jesus, Thy blood and righteousness
> My beauty are, my glorious dress;
> Midst flaming worlds, in these arrayed,
> With joy shall I lift up my head.
>
> Bold shall I stand in that great day,
> Cleansed and redeemed, no debt to pay;
> Fully absolved through these I am
> From sin and fear, from guilt and shame.
>
> (Nicholas von Zinzendorf)

May the Lord Jesus be unto you your Righteousness.

Be Encouraged!

Why Wallow When You Can Worship?

Bless the Lord, O my Soul, and all that is within me,
bless His holy Name.
Psalm 103:1 KJV

Friend,

What do you do when things don't go your way? I mean, when things are tough, and it would be really easy to just sit in the mire of self-despair?

What about when that dreaded "friend" Melancholy taps on the window of your soul and begs for an invite in?

Or, when someone speaks to you in a manner that pretty well rips the heart right out of you, how do you respond?

When your family members, or workmates, are having bad days, how do you respond to their *un*pleasantries towards you? Do you "give as good as you get" or worship Jesus through responding in kindness and love?

Which option do you choose when it would be far easier to be grumpy than gracious?

On those days when you just seem to get up on the wrong side of the bed, and sourness seems like the only mood appropriate for the day before you, do you leave your soul to wallow in the slough of self-indulgent irritability, or do you bow to the Lordship of Jesus Christ *even over your moods* and determine to worship Him with your attitude that day?

Countless times a day, in every venue of our lives, we are given the choice to honour God or serve our flesh; to move to the Majesty or to the mud; to Worship or Wallow.

Now, it is *always* easier to wallow like a pig in the sty of self-pity, or resentment, or irritability, or grumpiness, or silence, or moodiness, or depression. It takes no faith, no fight, no forgiveness to wallow.

Anyone can do it. It is purely natural. It takes no grace to be a grumbler, no faith to be a fusser, no prayer to be a party-pooper, no reverence to be a resenter.

Wallowing feels good because it indulges the flesh. When that mud squelches up between the toes, there is a satisfaction in the familiarity of the pigsty. But remember: it is filth that is "comforting" you.

Wallowing is sin. Call it nothing less. Face it for what it is; be tough on yourself for indulging your flesh in the muck. John Piper writes: "God threatens terrible things on those who grumble." (*c.f.* Psalm 106:25-26).

Murmuring dishonors God who promises to work all things together for our good (Romans 8:28). Complaining puts out the light of our Christian witness (Philippians 2:14-15). A critical, anxious spirit dries up joy and peace (Philippians 4:6-7).

Now, I confess that I have been a wallower for much of my life. I have often found solace in worry, or moodiness, or resentment. There is a strange comfort in various forms of misery. But I have grown increasingly convicted that my wallowing is a dishonour to the God who calls me to worship and gives grace to follow the call.

While I've still got mud between my toes, I have learned that:

*It is a sin for me to be irritable when my God wills for His Joy to be complete in me.

*It is a sin to give into the flesh and be as negative as those around me, giving as good as I get, when God calls me to be salt and light in my world.

*It is a sin to pull a mood when the Lord Jesus is calling us to be His witnesses, which, for me, includes loving my wife as Christ loves His Church, and my neighbour as myself.

But to worship ... to WORSHIP ... to grab hold of my soul and tell it to "Forget not all His benefits," (Psalm 103:2 KJV)to order my inner being to "bless [praise] His holy Name," (Psalm 103:1 KJV) to "Lift my eyes to [Him] whose throne is in Heaven," (Psalm 123:1)to say with the Psalmist: "Why are you downcast, O my soul?" [in other words, "Why are you wallowing?"] "Put your hope in God, for I will yet praise Him." (Psalm 42:11) ... rather than wallow is a God-honoring response to the grace which God avails to us every day. It:

*Strengthens the soul

*Encourages those around us

*Discourages the Enemy

*Declares to the World the supremacy and goodness of Christ.

Wallowing is sin.

Worshipping is the only fitting response of a redeemed soul.

Is it time YOU stopped wallowing and started worshipping?

I'll leave you with a truth about God just to help you out of the mud and on your way to the Majesty:

The Lord Your God is with you, He is mighty to save. He will take great delight in you, He will quiet you with His love,He will rejoice over you with singing. (Zephaniah 3:17).

Yours, leaving the mud puddle, in Jesus.

Be Encouraged!

Filled ... But Still Room For More!

Be [being] Filled With the [Holy] Spirit.
Ephesians 5:18

Dear Miracles,

Did you know that every believer in Jesus Christ *is* a miracle, called by Christ from sin and death to life and godliness?

I want to encourage us toward seeking and living a life of supernatural power and purpose. I want to encourage us towards the Spirit Filled life.

Now, immediately I am betraying my charismatic convictions. While I firmly believe that every believer in Jesus has the Holy Spirit residing within him, I see everywhere in the Scriptures, and all about me in Christian experience, the reality that there is a fullness for which we must yearn, a filling for which we must ask.

I could marshal no end of Bible passages to support this belief, but I will simply draw your attention to the one at the top of this page: Ephesians 5:18. It reads in the NIV "... be filled with the Spirit," but the literal translation is "... be *being* filled with the Holy Spirit." In other words, it speaks of an ongoing filling, or, if you will, an ongoing *being filled*.

One could describe the Spirit Filled life as a life of "be being filled-ness."

Now this command, to "be being filled" was written to people who were already believers in Jesus. Certainly they already were born again by the Holy Spirit, and had His Presence. The Bible tells us as much:

Having believed, you were marked in Him with a seal, the promised Holy Spirit. (Ephesians 1:13).

Is that not enough?Why the command for an ongoing filling?Why should I seek the Lord for an increased fullness?

Why did Paul pray that the Ephesians would be *"filled to the measure [with] all the fullness of God"* ?(3:19)

Well, I have been to college and university and seminary, and I can talk theological talk, and lecture using fancy words, but really, my theology of the Holy Spirit, and the answer to the above questions, can be summed up in the following statement:

I Need Him and I Leak!

I want to live a *super*natural life that brings honour and glory to Jesus Christ. I don't want to hug the shore, but I want to put out to the deep waters. I want to be full of the Lord Jesus, and I want to love and live in ways impossible without the Lord. I want to see the darkness dispelled by the Light of Jesus Christ shining from my life and from the Church of which I am a part.

I want to Burn for Christ ... not just exist.

Now, I trust that you want the same. I cannot imagine being a Christ-Follower, and wanting anything less. And so, I/we need the present filling of God's Holy Spirit. He is indispensable in lives that are to be lived in Time, but for the sake of Eternity.

So, what is the secret of "be being filled-ness?" What do *we* do in order to put ourselves in the place where God will do what *He* promises to do? I want to give you four simple (but not easy!) steps. Credit goes to A.W. Tozer's *Keys to the Deeper Life, "Brimming Over With the Spirit."*

Each step is vital, and, if employed with all our hungry hearts, will lead to lives of "be being filled-ness."

---

1) **Surrender**. Romans 12:1 tells us that in view of God's mercy we are to offer our very bodies as living sacrifices. There *MUST* be surrender to the Lordship of Jesus Christ if there is to be fullness! He who will be our Master will not be our mascot! We need to be giving our lives over to the Lordship of Jesus Christ daily.

2) **Ask.** Luke 11:13 reminds us that if *we* being "evil, know how to give good gifts to [our] children, *how much more* will the Lord give the Holy Spirit to those who *ask* Him!" (emphasis added). Asking implies humbling ourselves. It implies a recognition of emptiness, and a confession of desperate need. Proud people ask for nothing and get it.

3) **Believe**. Galatians 3:2 tells us that we receive the Holy Spirit by *hearing with faith.* Friend, our Heavenly Father longs to fill us. Jesus wants us to live an abundant life (John 10:10). He wants to give us power to be His witnesses (Acts 1:8). Fullness is not for the "spiritually elite," but for each and every one of us. If we would be being filled, we need to believe that our Father is ready and willing to do so!

4) **Obey**. Acts 5:32 insists that God gives the Holy Spirit to those who obey Him. God will not anoint our rebellion. He does not empower us so that we can be naughty. He gives us of Himself so that we can live for the honour and glory of His Son. A life of repentance towards obedience is assumed in a life of "be being filledness."

Now, I don't intend to reduce the miraculous to a mere formula. As I said, the above four may be simple to grasp, that is, not complex to understand, but that does not mean they are *easy* to *do*! To *Surrender*, to *Ask*, to *Believe,* to *Obey*, these four mean death to the Self-Life and a readiness to live and suffer for Christ and His Gospel....

But! What is the option? A life of comparative futility.Forever striving in one's own strength. Being continually frustrated by one's lack of Joy and Life. Hugging the shore when the call is to the deep. Living as paupers when we are called to be sons. Wasting the years instead of serving the King.

Fellow Follower, let's get before our God, and putting our Self-Life on the altar, let's exchange it for His Spirit-Life, that we may live *super*natural lives for the Glory of God.

Yours Saved, and Safe, Satisfied, but still hungry for more of Jesus,

Be Encouraged!

We Know Who is in Charge Here

His Kingdom rules over all.
Psalm 103:19

The insurance companies called it "An Act of God." I'll go with that.

To attribute the 2010 volcanic explosion in Iceland to the Sovereign God of the Universe is thoroughly biblical.

... He lifts His voice, the earth melts. (Psalm 46:6)

Come and see the works of the Lord, the desolations He has brought on the earth. (Psalm 46:8)

... His Kingdom rules over all ... (Psalm 103:19)

Yes, indeed, the world of the Bible (which is the world I choose to live in) is a world not of chance, or luck, or coincidence, but a deliberate world in which an Everlasting Holy God:

... works out everything in conformity with the purpose of His will ... (Eph 1:11)

... bring[s] all things in heaven and on earth together under one head, even Christ. (Eph. 1:10)

So, let's let an Icelandic volcano be "An Act of God." Here is what happened:

The Sovereign Lord of the Universe, who has one great purpose, which is to bring Glory to Himself, through His Son, in the redeeming, subduing, and renewing of a wayward, proud, rebellious planet which we call Earth ... scraped the top off a mountain in Iceland (like we would pick a scab with our fingernail) and in so doing, all but shut down a proud, godless continent of proud, godless men and women.

Indeed!

Industries were threatened. People were in a stranded panic.

Commerce stumbled.

Even the presidents and princes had to oblige the "Act of God" and stay home!

It just does not take much for God to subdue us when He wants to.

Indeed!

... He thwarts the purposes of the peoples ... (Psalm 33:10)

God reigns over the nations. (Psalm 47:8)

The Lord is exalted over all the nations. (Psalm 113:4)

Now, you may not buy into this. You may prefer to live in a world of

Chance ...

Luck ...

Happenstance ...

In which case events such as this volcano (and earthquakes, and cancer, and tribulations, and worse) have little or no redeeming value. They just "happen" to occur quite without the purpose of God, and perhaps even to His surprise.

But I cannot live in such a world. I need the Bible World of meaning and purpose governed by a Good, Holy God. Hence, I need to *learn* and *take heed* from all events, even a volcano, being reminded of the smallness of *me*, and the greatness of the Lord.

As I sat and watched the unfolding news of the eruption from the comfort of my father's lounge in Kansas, wondering if, and when, I would return home to the UK, I, along with my wife, was certainly aware of how *my* plans were completely subject to God and His acts. How proud, arrogant, sure of myself/ourselves I/we quickly become! I need to hear and heed the words of James, the half-brother of Jesus:

Now listen, you who say, 'Today or tomorrow we will go to this or that city...carry on business, and make money.' Why you do not even know what will happen tomorrow. What is your life? You are a mist that appears for a little while and then vanishes. Instead, you ought to say, 'If it is the Lord's will we will live and do this or that.' As it is, you boast and brag. All such boasting is evil. (James 4:13-16)

Our arrogance is not only foolish, it is evil. We will do well to allow such events to *humble* us, and *magnify* God. In our over-confidence we need to be put in our place, and place our trust in our unshakable God who is over all. Chances are that our culture, in the main, won't get the message from this (or any other) "Act of God," but that doesn't mean that *we* cannot.

God rules over the ways of arrogant man. We will do well to remember this, for there is a greater shaking coming. It may not be far off, for He has promised:

Once more I will shake not only the earth, but also the heavens...so that that which cannot be shaken may remain. (Hebrews 12:26,27)

If His fingernail can subdue a continent, what will become of us when He bares *"His holy arm"* ?(Psalm 98:1)

Where is your confidence?

Where is your hope?

Who holds certainty for you?

Therefore, since we are receiving a Kingdom that cannot be shaken, let us be thankful, and so worship God acceptably with reverence and awe, for our 'God is a consuming fire.' (Hebrews 12:28,29)

Yours, under a Sovereign God.

Be Encouraged!

We Are Resurrection People

I want to know Christ, and the power of His resurrection.
Philippians 3:10

Dear Resurrection People,

How Glorious,
      Liberating,
            Empowering,
                  it is to be followers of the Risen Lord Jesus!

I long for us to be affected to the very centre of our beings with the power of the Resurrection.

We can be ... The Bible says so:

> *We were therefore buried with Him through baptism into His death in order that just as Christ was raised from the dead ... we too may live a new life.* (Romans 6:4)

> *I want to know Christ, and the power of His resurrection.* (Philippians 3:10)

> *I pray ... that you may know ... His incomparably great power... the working of His mighty strength which He exerted in Christ when He raised Him from the dead.* (Ephesians 1:18-20)

The power of His Resurrected Life is to be ours, and is to permeate every aspect of our beings. To this end, it is my concern that there be no dark corners in our lives where the light of the Risen Jesus is not permitted to shine ... that there be no secret compartments where sin is left unchecked to smolder until it gets its opportunity to flame.

This is a most serious issue. We must allow and invite the Lord Jesus to be Lord of *every* area of our lives. We must allow Him - in His Risen Glory - to bring light and life into every room, every closet, every nook and cranny. Otherwise unchecked sin will breed in the dark areas until it has its chance ... And then it will have us.

I cannot be two (or more) people. We cannot want the power of Christ's resurrection in some parts of our lives and not in others, on Sunday morning but not on Friday night, in public but not in private. There cannot be a "secret me." I have to be the same man in all circumstances. I must play at all times to an audience of one: The Risen Lord Jesus. A secret sin can become my strange companion. I can seek solace in it when things get me down, retreating on tough days into my murky corner of:

Lust ...
Gossip ...
Jealousy ...
Alcohol ...
Porn ...
Gambling ...
Flirting ...
Lying ...
Eating ...

... there receiving a perverse "comfort."

It can progress until I cannot imagine how I could do without my shadowy "friend" ... growing hardened to the thought of Jesus being Lord over that one area.

But there will always be a price to pay.

Let me tell you a tragic and true story:

My friend is a pastor in the USA. Among his duties, he has pastoral care over a young family: Father, mother, and infant. It appeared to be a beautiful Christian home, and in many ways, it was.

But the young father had a sinister secret.

He was exploring pornography on the internet.

It began small, but grew and grew, until he could not control himself.

He began to indulge his lusts in ways he never imagined he would, or could.

He ended up communicating with a 15 year old girl over the internet.

Only it was not a 15 year old girl, it was a police officer, and this young husband and father was busted in a "sting" operation and went to prison ... He will be locked up for years.

Friends, as Resurrection People there can be no secrets in our lives; no unconfessed sin; no private closets of wickedness.

Not one of us knows where secret sin will take us, but it will not be to a good place.

... and you may be sure that your sin will find you out. (Numbers 32:23)

Beloved, "it is for freedom that Christ has set us free." (Galatians 5:1) Let us be joyful followers of the Risen Lord Jesus. But let us not play games with His Lordship. There is simply no escaping the consequences of our choices: Joyful consequences for obedience, tragic consequences for hypocrisy.

Pray this prayer with me:

Lord Jesus, I praise you for being the Risen Lord and my Saviour. I invite you, with all my heart, to be Lord of *every* area of my life. Lord! May there be no "secret me!" May I play to You as my Audience whether I be before others or in private. Cause me to fear secret sins. Cause me to hate whatever You hate, and to love whatever You love.

Make me see the beauty of holiness of heart and life, and the joy of obedience. Risen Lord, shine your light into the secret corners of myself. Lead me to confess my exposed sins before your Cross, and give me the grace I will need to hate them and to Love You.

For the Joy set before me, give me grace to follow hard after You, and to forsake all that would bring dishonour to Your Precious Name, hurt to my precious soul, and hurt to countless other tender souls.

Grace and Peace as we together pursue the Risen Christ as our Prize.

Yours in faith, but with fear and trembling.

Be Encouraged!

Here is a Feast for Your Soul

*May the God of Hope fill you with all joy and peace as you trust
in Him, so that you might overflow with hope by the power of the
Holy Spirit.*
Romans 15: 13

Dear Friend in Hope,

One of the blessings I often receive from the Bible is when a
particular Scripture, perhaps just a verse or two, really reaches into
my heart and experience. When this happens, I can often "feed" on
that passage for days at a time, considering its nuances and surprises,
discovering its flavours and textures, as it reveals to me new and
wonderful things about our Great God and Saviour. At such times
my soul is truly nourished by the Lord Himself, through His Word.

One such Scripture is found near the end of the book of
Romans. Having already fed upon the great truths available in that
rich book, it would be easy to pass over the feast available in
chapter15, verse13. But a delight for the soul awaits us there, and we
will do well not to pass over it too quickly:

*May the God of Hope fill you with all joy and peace as you trust in
Him, so that you might overflow with hope by the power of the Holy
Spirit.*

Now that little verse is loaded with goodness. We could feed
our souls upon it for days and not finish it off. Let's consider it -
chew on it - together for just a little while.

First, this is a benediction from the Apostle Paul to the sisters
and brothers in Rome. In these words, he is pronouncing a blessing
upon his beloved Christian family. He is revealing his heart's desire

---

for his fellow followers of Jesus Christ. Now, it will be in no way rude of us to hold out our plates and say "Hey! Can I have a bit of this blessing too?" I am sure that Paul will say "Plenty for everyone! Come and dine!", as he heaps our plates as well as those of his friends in Rome.

These words of blessing are for us too! Receive them and begin to feast upon them.

First, notice how he describes God: *"The God of Hope."* What a description of God! The biblical word "hope" is a strong word, not a weak word. It speaks of confident expectations of good things to come. It speaks of a bright tomorrow. I can face tomorrow certain of good things ordained and planned by God, because He Himself is the very author of Hope.

Dwell upon who God is described to be in these words. Meditate on the words *"God of Hope."*

Notice with me that little word right at the start *"May."* Even this is significant. It speaks of a willing disposition within this *"God of Hope"* to act on our behalf. Paul does not say "perhaps" or "if," but *"May."*

And just what is Paul confident that this *"God of Hope"* will do for us? *"Fill us with all joy and peace"* as we trust in Him. Oh what words of power! Divine Joy and Peace come from the Eternal God Himself and are not dependent upon events fixed in space and time. Open up your heart and receive this blessing! Fullness of Joy and Peace! This is Paul's heart for those in Rome, and for us as well, even for all who are in Christ. But more, this is *God's heart* behind Paul's heart.

"As you trust in Him." Beloved, settle the matter now! Be sure of God's heart in this. Believe God about this. God *wants* to fill you with Joy and Peace. He is *disposed towards you* to do so. Don't let the sin of unbelief rob you of the blessing that God wishes to bestow upon you. We can miss countless blessings if, through unbelief, we opt for the easy low life of sin when God is calling us to the heights with Him.

But there is more! Get ready to receive yet *more*. *"So that you might overflow with hope."* This is *beyond fullness*. This means that we become channels of hope for others. *Overflowing with hope.* Don't you want this to be your experience? God wants to make you a channel of His hope for a hopeless world around you. Think about this: You (!) a river of *Hope*. Instead of being a grumpy, morose source of gloom, can you imagine being a person who touches every life around you with God-given hope? Believe it. Don't settle for less. Refuse a hopeless "no" face, and receive a hope-filled "yes" face.

"By the power of the Holy Spirit." It is not up to us. This is *super*natural. This is from God. We trust in Him; He works in us. That is the way it goes. It is not about "me being positive," but about God being faithful and empowering me to be a hope-filled, joy-filled, peace-filled source of blessing to those around me. It is about me having nothing but *emptiness,* Jesus having nothing but *willingness to fill*, and me receiving. As Charles Spurgeon once said, the best saints are simply the best receivers.

I will leave you now to continue your feast, until your soul is satisfied in Christ. My only plea is that you determine to settle for nothing short of what God has for you in Jesus Christ.

Yours hungry for the Feast.

Be Encouraged!

Our Freedoms Are Founded in Jesus

I urge then, first of all, that requests, prayers, intercession and thanksgiving be made for everyone - for kings and all those in authority, that we may live peaceful and quiet lives in all godliness and holiness. This is good and pleases God our Saviour, who wants all men to be saved and come to a knowledge of the Truth.
1Timothy 2:1-5

Dear Church,

As I write this letter, I am supposed to be teaching a group of pastors here in Port au Prince, Haiti. But, there is an election taking place. Hence, the complimentary rioting, burning, and killing (yes) in the streets. So, here I am stuck in my room ... too dangerous to venture out.

Now, I was in England for the General Election of 2010. I marveled at it then, and I marvel at it now even more so. Let me try to explain:

I think few appreciated what had transpired before their eyes. An election, fought between parties divided by deep ideological differences had given an inconclusive result. Days of uncertainty and negotiations behind closed doors ensued. Finally, as one government dissolved, a new one had been formed.

And there were no riots in the streets. No one had been beaten or killed. No blood had flowed.

Do we *realize* the profound rarity of such an occurrence in the annals of human history? Do we realize just how few countries on earth today, and throughout history, have had the moral framework to withstand such political uncertainty, turmoil, and shake-up without wheeling out the guillotine or the tanks? Are we appreciative of just *how long* it has taken those fair lands to reach such a blessed place?

But, more importantly, do we realize just how fragile, how thin, is the skin of civility and true humanity, and how close every culture, including Western culture, is to tyranny, cruelty, and anarchy?

And, more, do we *understand* the spiritual, intellectual, and cultural *REVOLUTION* which took place over the centuries, thus providing the foundation, the framework, for the civility and true "humanity" which we take for granted today?

Here is my observation: It is the penetration of Christianity deep into the very fabric, the "DNA" of England, over centuries, which has built the foundation and framework to support the values, the freedoms, the fairness which we all enjoy. It is Christianity that has given us "humanity," which has taught us of the value and integrity of every person before God, and which has, in so doing, opened the door for the social and cultural freedoms which we have come to expect and view as "normal."

But they are *not* normal. They are exceptional. They are fragile. They can decay and be gone in a moment. Most cultures, in most places, in most times, have been unimaginably inhumane.

And we are always only a generation away from an age of cruelty.

Here is my fear: As a Western country (proudly, arrogantly, stridently) moves into a "post-Christian" age, we will find ourselves moving, very surely and unstoppably, into a "post-human" age. The kind of political "miracle" which we observed in 2010 may one day be replaced by men in jack-boots with rifles, with the complimentary blood in the streets.

And here is my concern (this really vexes me): *No one sees this.* Our political leaders defiantly do not see the necessary link between Christianity and freedom. Surely, Christians have many times gotten it wrong. We have, shamefully, slain our thousands in being *un*faithful to Christ. But atheism and secularism have slain their *millions* in being *faithful* to their cause.

The popular "fundamentalist" atheists of the newsstand (Richard Dawkins and co.) are not bright enough to make the connection. The brighter atheists of yesteryear saw more clearly the necessary link between a post-Christian culture and a new age of tyranny. Thus Friedich Nietzsche, who died in 1900, (having first pronounced that God was "dead" before he went insane) rightly predicted that Europe would descend into a bloodbath, the 20th century being destined to be the bloodiest of all time.

Even our church leaders do not see that the compromising of the uniqueness of Christ and His Gospel - in a bid to build a "fairer Britain" - is nothing other than sawing off the branch they are sitting on. It is precisely Christ and His Gospel which produced the very idea and dream of fairness in the first place!

What are we to do? Begin with the Scripture at the head of this letter. We must *pray* for our leaders. God has established civil government for the common good of all people, and it is the particular calling of the Believers in the world to pray for "kings and all those in authority." We can pray that they may be of noble character and integrity. We can pray for God to save them and use them to His good purposes. We can plead for God to have mercy upon them and upon us as a nation.

More, *we* need to be people of deep integrity and Christian conviction. Shallowness and hypocrisy just won't do. A Holy Church is "salt and light" to a society. If we simply blend in with the godless culture around us, adopting their amoral attitudes, we fail our Lord, our generation, and the generations that follow us. Our *minds* need to be schooled by Jesus Christ; our *hearts* need to love Him above our personal comfort and prosperity; our *actions* need to be consistent with His Lordship over our lives. The best thing we can do for our culture is go deep with Jesus ourselves.

Finally, we need to evangelize. There is no other hope for the land than the conversion of hearts and lives, boys and girls, old and young, to Jesus. Only *He* can preserve a nation, and He does so one person at a time, one family at a time, one church at a time.

Beloved, we are *living* in a fragile miracle. It is called freedom. We dare not take it for granted, even if our leaders do.

May God Grant us grace and courage to live valiantly for Jesus Christ today.

Yours, and gratefully so.

Be Encouraged!

Jesus Himself Ensures Your Salvation

But now a righteousness from God, apart from the law, has been made known, to which the Law and the Prophets testify. This righteousness from God comes through faith in Jesus Christ to all who believe. There is no difference, for all have sinned and fall short of the glory of God, and are justified freely by his grace, through the redemption that came by Jesus Christ. God presented him as a sacrifice of atonement, through faith in his blood ... He did it to demonstrate his justice... so as to be just and the one who justifies those who have faith in Jesus.
Romans 3:21-26

Dear Friends,

Above is perhaps the most important, most marvelous paragraph ever penned.

Now, while this paragraph deserves detailed exploration (for it is certainly, if not the Everest, then the Matterhorn of Bible Truth), I really just want to use it as a springboard to spotlight what I am increasingly seeing as a real pastoral problem ... one which is certain to rob us of power for mission and life, and threaten the well-being of our churches. If the above passage speaks of anything, it speaks of the rock-solid *assurance* which a Believer can (and must) have in the light of the redeeming work of Jesus Christ. We discover in this passage that a "righteousness from God" has been put into effect (as opposed to any righteousness which we can generate); that this gifted righteousness is received solely "through faith in Jesus Christ" (as opposed to being via any works which we can produce). This righteousness is available to all for there is *"no difference, for all have sinned and fall short of the glory of God"* (as opposed to anyone having a natural, racial, cultural, or religious advantage). The entire saving work springs from the very heart of God, who "presented him [Jesus Christ] as a sacrifice of atonement ... so as to justify those who have faith in Jesus" (as opposed to it springing from any offering on our part to appease God).

The Gospel invites us to *REST* in Jesus and His Gospel. But here is the pastoral problem of which I am becoming increasingly aware:

I do not see an abundance of assurance regarding salvation in our midst. The result is a loss of power, a diminished joy, a nagging sense of legalistic guilt, a failure to Glory in Jesus Christ in all things and at all times.

Let me ask you:

*Are you at *rest* in Jesus and in the work which He has finished for your salvation?

*Do you *glory* in the Cross?

*Is there a deep assurance that Heaven is yours and that Christ Himself has secured it for you?

*Are you truly confident that your sins have been removed, placed upon Jesus Himself, and His righteousness has been given to you as a free gift?

*Do you realize that all of this is from God, who loved you first?

*Are you rejoicing today in the fact that since you could do nothing to earn His particular, electing love, so you can do nothing to lose it?

*Is there a love of holiness growing in you as a response to God securing you in His grace?

*Are you desiring to publish the fame of Him who sought you first and bought you with His own blood?

I recommend that you take prayerful time over these questions. Linger and labour over them until you can answer "yes" to each and every one of them. Be diligent with your soul, even as you are with your finances or hobbies, and it will bring you great reward.

Being able to see and affirm the above in a Christian's experience is the unique privilege of every true Believer. I believe it was the Puritan, John Owen, who said that the two biggest problems a pastor has are 1) getting sinners to believe that they are sinners, and 2) *getting the saved to believe that they are saved!*

Four things will prevent assurance from being deep and real in your life:

1) Not realizing that it is part of your birthright in Christ, a logical and necessary result of believing in the Gospel.

2) Failing to rest your hopes on Christ and His finished work, somehow believing that you have to produce your own righteousness to offer to God.

3) The cherishing of sin in one form or another (loving the world more than Christ), causing you to admit to yourself that you are not taking repentance from sin and faith toward Christ with true earnestness.

4) The mistaken notion that assurance will lead to laziness and complacency where discipleship and holiness is concerned.

A Believer needs to have a sure, yes even bold, confidence that he belongs to Jesus, to whom he has pledged his entire life and being. If you are lacking true Gospel assurance, search your heart and discover which of the above to be true of you. Deal with God and yourself in that area until you have a breakthrough into a new place of rest and peace with Christ. Do not settle for anything less.

Searchingly Yours,

Be Encouraged!

Christ Can Give You Heavenly Resolve

Teach us to number our days aright, that we might gain a heart of wisdom.
Psalm 90:12

Dear Fellow Pilgrim,

In 1722, 20 year old Jonathan Edwards of Connecticut, New England, began to draw up seventy "Resolutions" by which he determined to live his life before God. Upon completion, he read them once every week (for the rest of his life), holding his resolve to live fully for the Glory of God, the good of others, and the happiness of his own soul. He went on to become the foremost Christian thinker, preacher, and pastor of his day, and to develop, for the Glory of God, one of the greatest minds the world has since seen. His volumes are with us today, inspiring men and women across the world to live their whole lives to and for the Glory of God.

One of his resolutions, number six of the seventy, reads as follows:

Resolved, to live with all my might, while I do live.

Now take some time with me to walk around this young man's resolution. My hope is that perhaps the beauty and power of it may affect our lives, as it most certainly did his.

First of all, consider with me the *value* of such a resolution:

We can so easily waste our seconds, which soon become minutes, hours, days ... years ... a lifetime. It takes *resolve* to be diligent with ourselves. Most live far beneath their potential in Jesus Christ. The Lord has created us for *purpose*. But walking in purpose requires a determination, a discipline, a resolve to make every day ... dare I say every *moment* count. This is not legalism, but it is taking grace for all it is worth.

56

We can become tragic time-wasters without the resolve to "live with all our might, while we do live."

Next, consider the *focus* of such a resolution:

The focus is upon *life*. Edwards resolved to LIVE, as opposed to just exist. Eating, breathing, sleeping are all things that fish, dogs, and humans do equally well. But embracing *life* is so much more than just existing for a few years. Jesus came that we might have LIFE, not just animal existence. It takes resolve to say, "I am determined to seek and apprehend fullness of life, for this is what the Lord Jesus has for me. I refuse anything less." Lesser things must go, that we may grab hold of the greater thing.

We can exchange life for mere existence unless we resolve to "live with all our might, while we do live."

Then, look at the *wisdom* of such a resolution:

The young Edwards had the present in clear view as he resolved to "live with all his might" while he had a life to live. How many live in the mists of yesterday, or the dreamy wisps of a tomorrow that may never be! This young man determined to live in *today*. His resolution reminds me of the advice of another young man, Jim Elliott: "Wherever you are, be all there." He resolved to make each day count, knowing he could depend upon nothing further.

We can miss the potential of the moment if we do not resolve to "live with all our might, while we do live."

Finally, see the *reach* of such a resolution:

While recognizing the brevity of this life, it assumes another life to come. There is a whiff of Eternity in Edward's resolve. This life is brief and uncertain, but it is the foyer of True Life, so we best live it well, to the full. Today counts precisely because there is Eternity to come. We dare not waste today, because all Eternity is watching to see what we do in Time.

We can fail to appreciate Forever if we do not resolve to "live with all our might, while we do live."

The Psalmist prayed:

Teach us to number our days aright, that we might gain a heart of wisdom. (Psalm 90:12)

We do well to consider often the brevity of life, the certainty of death, the fact of our accountability to Jesus Christ, and the glories (and miseries) of Eternity. Such ponderings can help us to resolve to "live with all our might, while we do live." The day will come, and soon, when it will be too late to get serious with the things that matter, too late to mend that relationship, too late to get a heart for missions, too late to witness to the grace and love of Jesus Christ, too late to resolve anything.

Just a thought: Might there be regrets in Heaven … tears shed for wasted grace and shallow living? True, there are no tears in Heaven … that is, in the Final Heaven of Revelation chapter 21 … It is only in the New Heavens and the New Earth at the very end of this Age that God finally "wipes every tear from [our] eyes." (Rev 21:4) Could it be that previous to that Final Day, there may be tears of regret, even among those redeemed souls who, knowing the wonders of Salvation, have to face the regretful reality of wasted grace here in this life? … Just a thought. …

May we learn from a lad of but 20, young Jonathan Edwards, to:

Resolve, to live with all our might, while we do live.

Yours, For Eternity's sake.

Be Encouraged!

We Are Dust, But More

... for He knows how we are formed, He remembers that we are dust.
Psalm 103:14

Dear Dust,

Nathan was a lad from Looe, Cornwall. Soundly saved by the grace of Jesus while in his late teens, he celebrated his 40th birthday with his wife, Sonya, and family a few days before he died.

One of my dearest friends, Nathan did not possess a "religious" bone in his body.

A faithful husband. A loving father. A committed pastor.

A diligent theologian. A street-level, weight lifting "bloke."

A worshipper of Jesus. My theological sparring partner.

He applied himself earnestly to the discovery of truth. Being significantly (and humorously) dyslexic, he had to work harder than most to learn of Christ. Trained as a plasterer, following his conversion to Jesus he could be found with his Bible out at break times ... right on the work site. He became one of the most well-read men I knew. The possessor of a keenly trained and finely honed mind, he eclipsed me, and most of our colleagues, at nearly every turn.

He could not stand theological sloppiness. He could not understand a pastor who did not love the pursuit of Truth. He had no ambition in life other than to love Jesus and His Church (he *did* daydream of drumming for Led Zeppelin, but that's another story ...)

When first diagnosed with the cancer that would kill him, I remember him telling me that he was not going to "waste" this cancer ... If he had to have it, it was going to be used for the good of his soul.

59

The last time I saw him was about ten days before he died. He (with his one remaining eye) was reading Henry Scougal's *The Life of God in the Soul of Man* (Several of us were reading through it together and reflecting upon it to one another over the internet). With glee he opened up to a given passage: "Look at this," he said, "Here is the heart of the book." (To my joy, I had underlined the very passage he had highlighted, agreeing with him that indeed it constituted the heart of Scougal's work.)

The passage read as follows:

"The worth and excellency of a soul [that is, a soul's health] *is to be measured by the object of its love. He that loveth mean and sordid things doth thereby become base and vile; but a noble and well-placed affection doth advance and improve the spirit unto a conformity with the perfections which it loves."* (In other words, you become like the thing you love.)

Like an athlete 'rounding that last bend of the track with the finish line in sight, Nathan was running to break the tape and win the prize! Trivial matters, sinful affections, foolish distractions ... had lost their grip. Suffering had pressed him to Jesus.

Staring his demise right between the eyes had done a purifying work in him.

He was focused, peaceful, "In the Zone."

It is not hard for me to imagine him now in "Paradise", with the wonder of a kid at Christmas, seeking out and chasing down John Calvin, under the smiling gaze of Jesus Himself.

But the impact upon me of his brief life and untimely death has caused me to consider the brevity of my own life. I am challenged myself to live these days with the very same resolve and focus that I saw in my dear friend through the years, as well as in the last year, weeks, and days of his life.

*Why should I not live as earnestly, everyday, as I saw him live out his days?

*Is not Eternity a mere heartbeat away for each and every one of us?

*Should not we be done with the trivial, the foolish, the petty?

*Are we not all dangerously, wondrously, *near* to that moment when we shall shed our mortal frames and fly away?

*Is not the veil thinning with every breath?

Beloved, we will do well to recall here Edward's *Resolution*:

RESOLVED, TO LIVE WITH ALL MY MIGHT, WHILE I DO LIVE.

Here's another great truth, this time from Jim Elliot, martyred at 28 by the Auca Indians:

MAKE SURE WHEN IT COMES TIME FOR YOU TO DIE, ALL YOU HAVE TO DO IS DIE.

Nathan was already running well when sickness and death began to chase him down. The die was cast, his direction was sure, his course was set. The trial only served to sharpen his spirit, lengthen his stride, deepen his resolve to finish well. Nothing of substance had to change in the man.

May it not be that we be found unprepared when comes *our* turn to be confronted with *our* unavoidable mortality. May we be living *now* for Christ, for His Kingdom, even while we have health and breath. May we heed the warnings and learn the lessons from the passing of those around us whom we know and love. May we not squander grace, embracing sin and self in exchange for Christ and His Kingdom.

Guard your soul, dear friend ... You are going to spend Eternity with it.

Your fellow follower.

61

Be Encouraged!

God Will Be Sure You Get Busted!

... and you may be sure that your sin will find you out.
Numbers 32:23

Dear Friends,

I received a letter in the post addressed to:

"Dr. John Gillespie"

Now, not really being one for titles, and preferring simply the biblical description of "Pastor," I do not often get letters addressing me as "Doctor."

My interests were aroused ...

Could it be that someone, perhaps from some great university or mission centre, had heard something of me and wanted my services?

Perhaps it is a request from ... distant Australia, or exotic Vancouver for me to come and speak. I opened the letter with a sense of anticipation. It was from the "Devon and Cornwall Constabulary"... the "cops." Did they want me to preach the gospel to their prisoners? Instruct their officers in biblical principles for interpersonal relationships?

I read on:

Dear Sir,

Vehicle Registration Number LSO4 YKM

In accordance with Section 1 of the Road Traffic Offenders Act of 1988, I hereby give you notice that it is intended to take proceedings against the driver of the above motor vehicle for the alleged offence of:

62

Contravening red traffic light

This allegation is supported by Photographic Evidence

BUSTED!

Now, I remember the event. I was late and lost, trying to get to a pastoral meeting. The light had *just turned.* It was *barely* red! I looked both ways, was really careful - honest, I was! I did not see any cars coming ... including any police cars ... So I made what I thought was a "smart move" and proceeded through the intersection, not recklessly, but "prudently."

Of course I could have stopped, if I really needed to. I was in complete control. (A fact which I thought made me *less* guilty, when in fact it made me *more* so.) I knew I had broken the law, but (I figured) I am basically a good guy, a law abiding citizen, and a careful driver. No one got hurt. What's the big deal?

Convinced that I had made a good move, and gone unnoticed, I didn't think about it again ...

Until I opened the letter addressed to "Dr. John Gillespie."

My first response to the letter was a mixture of anger and self-justification: There must be some mistake! How was I to know there was a camera? I did not see one ...

Besides, I was on a "mission of mercy!" Don't they know what a good driver I usually am?

Can't they just ignore this one, just once? Now I have to pay a nice fine and get three points on my license.

BUMMER

This little episode has reminded me of a few "home truths" regarding the nature of sin:

1.   Usually we can stop, but choose not to.

63

2.	Usually, we find ways to convince ourselves that our transgressions are uniquely justifiable.

3.	Usually, the sinful behaviours which we justify in ourselves would outrage us if we found them in others.

4.	Usually we forget about the act once a bit of time has passed, but the fact of the transgression remains none-the-less.

5.	Usually, we convince ourselves that "no one saw it," and that "no one got hurt", and that therefore it did not matter anyway.

6.	Inevitably **we get caught**. .

Sin is deceptive. It is a transgression of God's Law, and, any way you look at it, God cannot overlook it. His very nature will not allow Him to, and the well being of the Universe which he made, loves, and governs depends upon Him pursing and prosecuting all transgressors. We run God's Red Lights willfully, arrogantly, dangerously, foolishly, to our own peril, and to the peril of our neighbours. God is too loving to let us get away with it.

I am afraid that where the Devon and Cornwall Constabulary are concerned, there is no one to pay my fine and take my penalty points upon themselves in my place. I'll have to bear the penalty myself.

Thankfully, where God is concerned, He has provided One who:

"knew no sin to be a sin offering for us." (2 Corinthians 5:21).

If, in the future, you see a VW Passat, registration # LSO4 YKM, know that I am driving really carefully, especially at red lights.

Yours Carefully,

Be Encouraged!

God Is Ready To Give More

And this is my prayer: That your love may abound more and more in knowledge and depth of insight, that you may be able to discern what is best and may be pure and blameless until the day of Christ, filled with the fruit of righteousness that comes through Jesus Christ - to the glory and praise of God.
Philippians 1:9-11

Dear Family,

Have you ever wondered how to pray for your church? One of the most helpful guides for your prayers is the New Testament, and, specifically, the prayers that the Apostle Paul prayed for the churches he loved and served. When we pray the very words of Scripture, we can be sure that we are praying according to God's will.

The prayer at the top of this letter is a prayer that Paul prayed for his beloved faithful fellow followers at Philippi (say that three times, real fast!). It unlocks for us the heart of the Apostle, and the heart of God for these dear saints at Philippi. (By the way, this same prayer can be applied to your family and friends.)

Walk through it with me, and then, please make it a part of your prayer life for your church, and for your family and friends.

Paul is not praying for surface issues. He is going deep. He prays for "abounding love." The New American Standard Version enhances the passage, bringing out its depth and colour:

That your love may abound still more and more in real knowledge and all discernment.

It is clear that these Philippians already have love abounding (that is, in abundance) toward God and each other, but Paul is praying for "still more and more." Pray that for your church! "Still More" and then, "and more." Now that is powerful praying that reached right into the very heart of God!

Pray that!

And Paul is not praying for mere sentimental love, but for love grounded in the Gospel. He prays for love founded in "knowledge and depth of insight." He does not want shallow believers, but educated followers of Jesus Christ who know Truth and whose love springs from a well of true Gospel understanding and "all discernment."

Pray that!

The Apostle's hope is that these dear Philippians, as they grow and abound in this genuine, knowledge-rich love, will be able to:

Discern what is best and be pure and blameless until the day of Christ.

Get this with me: Love which is already abundant, being made to be "still more" and then "more" abundant, founded upon true knowledge and understanding, deep in insight and wisdom, producing the ability to "discern what is best," leading to "pure and blameless" lives until Jesus comes back or death calls away!

Wow! Pray that!

But there is more. Along the way, we are to be not just abounding "still more and more" in love, and genuine knowledge, living pure and blameless lives (that would be wonderful in itself!), but Paul prays that the Philippians may be:

… filled with the fruit of righteousness that comes through Jesus Christ.

———

66

"Filled with fruit!" Even more than one of my wife's apple pies which bursts forth with an abundance of fruit, that word "filled" literally means "*being* filled." In other words, it is an ongoing experience of fullness from deep within, right from the soul, not just on the surface. It is not a veneer of goodness, but a deep fullness of righteousness, whose source can be none other than Jesus Christ Himself.

Pray that!

Finally, that all of this abounding, "still more" and then "more" abounding love, bringing forth pure, knowledgeable, fruitful lives, may result in:

> *... the glory and praise of God.*

How could it result in anything else? What else could a true church hope for, than that their lives *together* end up redounding to the "glory and praise of God?"

Pray that!

Let me leave you with *The Message* translation of this passage, because it faithfully brings out its richness. May you be encouraged to pray this passage into reality in your church and family.

So this is my prayer: That your love may flourish and that you will not only love much but well. Learn to love appropriately. You need to use your head and test your feelings so that your love is sincere and intelligent, not sentimental gush. Lead a lover's life: circumspect and exemplary, a life Jesus will be proud of: bountiful in fruits from the soul, making Jesus Christ attractive to all, getting everyone involved in the glory and praise of God.

May the Lord Jesus encourage by the Scriptures to pray His very heart for His Church.

Yours Praying.

Be Encouraged!

You Have Been Chosen By Grace

You did not choose me, but I chose you ...
John 15:16

Dear Church,

In 1975 I was apprehended by Jesus Christ.

When it happened, I thought that "I had decided to follow Jesus," and, from my vantage at that time, I had.

But looking back on it now I see that He, the Eternal Son of God - moved by nothing outside of Himself, compelled by nothing in me except need - sovereignly and mercifully apprehended me by His grace ... for His glory and for my good.

I became His possession. In biblical terms, Jesus:

Purchased me

Ransomed me

Rescued me

Redeemed me

Took hold of me

His purpose in this was that I might:

Know Him

Glorify Him

Enjoy Him

Honour Him

At that time He promised to:

Cleanse me

Keep me

Change me

Fill me

Use me

Delight in me

That I might:

Be satisfied in Him

Walk with Him

Magnify Him

Worship Him

That was 40 years ago. And He has been endlessly faithful to me. Many times I have:

Forgotten Him

Denied Him

Ignored Him

Disappointed Him

But He has always given me yet more grace to:

Return to Him

Confess to Him

Open up to Him

Seek Him

Be renewed in Him

Rejoice again in Him

Walk again with Him

As I look to the future, He promises to:

Give me all the grace I need to love and serve Him

Keep me until the end

Make my dying day a day of triumph

Keep me safe through the day of God's wrath

Present me faultless before His Father's Throne

Invite me into His Eternal Glory

I am so glad that I belong to Jesus!

Yours and eternally thankful.

Be Encouraged!

God's Heart Longs for Yours

As the deer pants for streams of water,
so my soul pants for you, my God.
My soul thirsts for God, for the living God ... Deep calls to deep.
Psalm 42:1,2,7

Thou hast made us for Thyself, O Lord, and our heart is restless until it finds its rest in Thee. (Augustine of Hippo)

Beloved,

I find that a precious marriage to a precious wife cannot satisfy my soul's thirst.

Seven wonderful children cannot speak peace to my inner restlessness.

A wonderful church full of dear fellow followers of Jesus cannot fill the void deep within.

My possessions,
    My hobbies,
        My friendships,
as wonderful as these are, betray a strange and growing desire for *something* which the best of this world simply cannot fulfill.

I find within my breast a deep yearning, what C.S. Lewis called an "Inconsolable Longing" of the soul.

Deep calls to Deep.

Now, don't misread me. I am eminently blessed of the Lord. My life has been, and remains, full and rich in innumerable ways. Yet, such blessedness only makes the longing more poignant, more pronounced.

I can feel alone, *truly alone* when all my loved ones are around me. I can feel dissatisfied, *deeply dissatisfied*, even with abundant wealth and all my material goods.

There is something in me that demands *more*, yes, even Eternity Itself, even God Himself. Solomon observed that God:

> ... *has also set eternity in the hearts of men.* (Ecclesiastes 3:11)

We all, as members of this fallen race, try to console, or subdue, or ignore, or appease our inconsolable selves. Some try to pretend the longing is not there. Some try to fill that longing with any one of an endless number of morsels and tidbits, but finally, to no avail.

What we need to do is to recognize that this inconsolable longing is in fact a dear friend. It is here to point us toward Him who alone can satisfy, to Him for whom we have been made. It is here to cast us upon the One who alone can meet the longing of our souls. Indeed, our souls are restless until they rest in Jesus Christ. It cannot be any other way. We have been made *by* Him, *for* Him. True Life begins when we finally, perhaps in bitter disappointment, realize the inability of all created things to truly satisfy, and begin to seek our satisfaction in Him who created all things. Such a realization, be it ever so unpleasant, is the doorway to Abundant Life.

C.S. Lewis astutely pointed out that just as the stomach and its hunger presupposes, yes demands, the existence of the food which alone can satisfy physical hunger, so the unseen self and its Inconsolable Longing presupposes, yes demands, another world beyond what is seen to satisfy its spiritual hunger. Don't expect your wife, or your job, or your hobby, or anything else in this visible, earthly realm to satisfy your Inconsolable Longing. It demands nothing less than Jesus and His Heaven. It is the meanest idolatry to look to any other than Jesus for that which none but He Himself can do .... namely, meet the deepest need of the God-shaped void in our souls.

The Inconsolable Longing can finally settle for nothing less than Jesus Christ. Not even His Book will do. Yes, it will get us started, keep us on the right way, and give us genuine glimpses of "Him whom our souls love," but in the end, we shall have to *see* and *have* ... Him. Hence, the true child of Grace is sometimes found with a faraway look in his eyes.

But, I cannot leave you without stretching to one final, and indeed more profound Truth. *Our* Inconsolable Longing may well be outdone by Another's. God Himself, in His Eternal Triune being - who has no needs within Himself - has *chosen* to need ... us. The evidence of the Bible is that Jesus has an Inconsolable Longing, one that may well involve you, and all of His Redeemed Ones:

Father, I want those you have given me to be with me where I am, and to see my glory, the glory you have given me because you loved me before the creation of the world. (John 17:24)

Our Inconsolable Longing corresponds to *His*. (WOW!) Consider this and embrace it. Your Longing will not go unfulfilled if you look to Him who Longs for you.

For He Longs that:

[His] Joy may be in [us]... and that [our] Joy may be complete. (John 15:11)

Again:

I am my Beloved's, and His desire is toward me. (Song of Songs 7:10 KJV)

Your Inconsolable Longing is God's deep call unto the depths of your soul. Hear and respond ... with all your being.

Fixed on this ground will I remain,
Though heart may fail and flesh decay;
This anchor shall my soul sustain
When earth's foundations melt away.
Mercy's full power I then shall prove,
Loved with an everlasting love!
  (Johann Rothe, 1727)

Yours, and Hungry for More.

Be Encouraged!

Your Entire Life is Nothing But Grace

*What do you have that you did not receive? And if you did receive it,
why do you boast as though you did not?*
1 Corinthians 4:7

Billy's Lemonade Stand

Billy wanted to make some money for a new dream bike and came up with the thought of a neighborhood lemonade stand.

He talked to his Dad about it, and Dad helped him plan out his stand. Billy's mom and dad loved it when Billy had ideas and dreams.

He got the wood he needed from his Dad's woodshed. Dad watched and helped as he cobbled his stand together.

Dad took him to the market and bought the lemons and sugar for him.

He went into his Mom's kitchen and she gave him all the jugs and cups he needed to stock his stand. She helped him make his lemonade.

Mom and Dad helped Billy put his stand together out by the street. He painted a sign using his father's paint and brushes: "Cold Lemonade! Only 10p!"

Dad was his first customer. Then Mom. Business was slow (recession!). Dad bought another glass of Billy's lemonade.

Mom had some friends over that day, and so she bought about five glasses. Her friends liked it so much, they brought their children over later and bought them each a glassful.

Billy's Dad had his buddies over to watch the football, so he (secretly) asked each of them to buy a glass of lemonade from Billy's stand.

Mom and Dad beamed as they watched Billy dream and work. By the end of the day Billy had sold all his lemonade!

Then, just to celebrate and reward a job well done, Mom and Dad took him out for ice cream, and for a gaze at his dream bike through the shop window.

Before bed that night, Billy hugged his parents and thanked them with all his heart for their goodness to him.

What a great day it had been! As he fell asleep he began dreaming of *two* lemonade stands ...

++

Beloved,

Have you considered (do we consider) the fact that *everything* we have and accomplish in our Christian life is solely the result of the grace and goodness of God? Billy's successful Lemonade stand (which is actually a story that was passed on to me from a wealthy businessman via my son-in-law, Jeff, expressing how he viewed his business success as being wholly due to the excessive goodness of God) was wholly the result of the goodness of his mom and dad.

Sure, Billy had an idea. But he lived in a home where ideas were encouraged. Of course he laboured. But his dad was right there guiding his hands. Dad and Mom supplied all that he needed. They were for him.

At the end of it all, they rewarded Billy with ice cream, never minding that the entire enterprise was built upon their generosity, their goodness, and their support. Billy could not help but overflow with love and thankfulness to his folks as the day came to a close.

So too, we who are citizens of God's Kingdom of Grace, need to be happily impacted by the fact that we live in a Kingdom where our ideas and dreams are *encouraged* by a loving and gracious Heavenly Father. He rejoices in our dreams. He is actually the source of them. He is ready to resource our efforts. He is there to guide our endeavours.He beams with joy as we stretch and try.

Even though He is the gracious provider and sustainer, and all our efforts are the result of His endless and boundless provision, He is happily excited to reward *us* (!) when our labours are finished.

This entire "economy of grace" results in an ever-increasing fellowship of love, thankfulness, dreaming, and stretching. The Kingdom of God is meant to be a Kingdom of Grace-empowered and fearless dreaming, stretching, trying, and rejoicing. We *must* model this and be a community where "GO FOR IT" is emblazoned on our hearts and faces.

Brothers and sisters, let's be sure that we allow the Lord to build every local church into an outpost of Heaven, where freedom, generosity of spirit, encouragement, and belief in one another are in the very air that we breathe.

Let's open up our hearts to the Lord and to each other and let God dream His dreams in and through us. The whole thing will result in God being yet more glorified, and our joy abounding.

Dream with me,

Be Encouraged!

God Gives All Grace for Faith and Patience

We do not want you to become lazy, but to imitate those who through faith and patience inherit what has been promised.
Hebrews 6:12

Brothers and Sisters in Christ,

I want you to notice with me two words in the above passage which we do not usually associate as belonging to each other: "faith" and "patience." In the wider passage, the writer is encouraging Hebrew Christians to press on following Jesus in the face of opposition and their own "fleshly" desires, warning them not to "cool off" in their discipleship, or, in his words, "become lazy."

Now, "becoming lazy" is not a danger unique to those first century followers. We too can be allured by our love of ease, familiarity, comfort, and our hatred of difficulties and unpopularity, to throttle back and put it into neutral, which the writer to the Hebrews would call being "lazy."

Now, the opposite of being "lazy" is being "zealous," that is, having love for Christ ablaze within our hearts. In order to ensure our maintenance of a burning heart, our passage encourages us to "imitate those who through faith and patience inherit what has been promised." He points us to former Christians - those who have already run the race, those who have already battled and beaten the opposition from without and within which urged them to "cool it." He speaks of the "faith and patience" which enabled them to persevere unto inheriting that which was promised.

Before we proceed, let's agree together that "what has been promised" can be nothing less, in the end, than Christ Himself and His Heaven.

In considering those noble saints who have gone before, I fear that by comparison, we have become a particularly fragile lot.

We pout easily. We quickly wave the white flag. It takes little to hurt our feelings. We too readily see ourselves as poor victims. We tend to be, what C.T. Studd called "chocolate soldiers" who quickly melt in the heat of battle. It will benefit us to consider those who have persevered well. That is why I find the reading of Christian (and sometimes secular) biographies to be so very helpful to my spiritual well-being. Reading of those who "through faith and patience" pressed on toward the prize rebukes my fragile desire to sulk in the corner and contemplate quitting.

So, on to these two words: "faith" and "patience." I find it interesting that the writer of the letter to the Hebrews sees these two qualities of the soul as being vitally linked. By considering their opposites, the connection between the two comes into sharp focus. Follow me: the opposite of "faith" is "unbelief."

The opposite of "patience" is, obviously, "impatience." Faith, (that is, confidence in the Living God, His promises and His character) cannot help but produce patience (that is, perseverance under trial) in the pursuit of "what has been promised." So, conversely, unbelief (that is, a lack of confidence in the Living God), cannot help but produce impatience (that is, quitting or going "lazy' when it gets tough) and a giving up in the pursuit of "what has been promised."

Therefore: As *Patience* is a first cousin of *Faith* ... So *Impatience* is a first cousin of *Unbelief.* Or: As *perseverance under trial* is a manifestation of *confidence in the Living God,* so *a penchant to quit or give up* is a manifestation of a *heart vote of "No Confidence"* in the living God. In practical terms, when I get impatient with my circumstances:

-with my wife, my family,

-my health,my church,

-my job,my lot in life,

I am, in brutal fact, registering my *un*belief. I am declaring through my impatience that God has not done a good enough job in my circumstances. My impatience is holding God Almighty in contempt, declaring that His Sovereignty over my life is suspect. Impatience is a manifestation of unbelief, and as such, is wicked sin! Conversely, when through faith we patiently persevere in:

-a difficult marriage, a thankless job,

-a joy threatening illness,a trialsome church situation,

-a difficult friendship,a challenging ministry calling,

we are, in wonderful truth, declaring with every heartbeat that we *believe* in the Lord God ... in His Providence over our lives, His ways, His leadings, His purposes.

Our patience *honours* Him!

Such "faith" and "patience" characterized earlier generations who, because they were confident in the goodness of the Lord, persevered:

-Even when the marriage was tough,

- or the health was broken,

-or the trial was endless.

They trusted all things to be useful toward their dying to self, and the conforming of themselves to the image of Christ.

And in so doing, they pressed on toward and inherited "what was promised."

Our unbelief – expressed in quitting, pouting, moaning, and feeling sorry for ourselves - is, in reality, nothing less than spiritual laziness, and, worse, a manifestation of contempt toward God Himself.

The antidote? 1) Recognize your impatient desire to quit and pout for what it is: a spiritually lazy, faithless, contemptuous heart. 2) Imitate those (learn from them, take inspiration from great and noble followers of Jesus) who through faith (confidence in the character and promises of God) and patience (perseverance under trial) gained their prize. 3) Never lose sight of "what has been promised," Jesus Himself and His Heaven.

Beloved, may those who will come after us look upon us as being numbered among those rare patient souls who confidently lived by faith in the Living God, that they may be inspired by our lives to live valiantly for Christ.

Yours … persevering.

Be Encouraged!

God is Glad When You Ask for More

How can I repay the Lord for all His goodness shown to me? I will lift up the cup of salvation and call upon The Name of the Lord.
Psalm 116:12-13

Beloved in Christ,

The goodness and mercy of God has left me hungry for more of Jesus.

That is what Grace always does ... It makes one hungry for yet more Grace. In fact, the only proper, God-glorifying response to Grace is to ask for more of it! Grace destroys the joy-killing deadly "debtor's ethic" that thrives in religion, but has no place in true Christianity.

Let me explain. The "debtor's ethic" basically says, "I owe you because you have been good to me." The natural world functions upon this principle, and really knows no other response to goodness.

It assumes that a debt can be paid and sets out to do so. But this is precisely why it can have nothing to do with Christianity. We can *never* repay the debt we owe to God, and to try is to reveal that we do not understand the Gospel in the first place. Yet many of us function upon the principle, spoken or unspoken (or sung, for many of our dearest hymns reflect the deadly "debtors ethic"), that we owe everything to God (true), and the rest of our lives will be our holy attempt to repay Him (false).

Think about that! Repay *Him*. As if we could! If we repaid The Lord, that would mean we had put ourselves on an even footing with the Almighty:

"There now, we are even. You saved me, and I paid you back with a faithful life. All is fair and square."

Or even worse:

"Okay God, you saved me. I have more than repaid you. I have lived an amazing life. Now you owe me."

The deadly "debtor's ethic" is the very antithesis of the life of Grace. It kills joy and produces either pride or despair.

Granted, yes, we *do* "owe" the Lord everything, for there is nothing we have that did not originate in His goodness. But this is not to presume that we can somehow repay Him or bring us to a place of level-pegging with the Almighty. Hence, the only true response to Grace is to ask for more! That is precisely what the Psalmist does in our verse at the top of this letter. He poses the question:

How can I repay the Lord for all his goodness to me?

And then he gives the only answer compatible with Grace:

I will lift up the cup of salvation and call upon the Name of the Lord.

In other words, he will raise a cup which the Lord has already from His Goodness filled, and *ask Him to fill it again!*

The Kingdom of God is oiled by the "Grace Ethic" and can have nothing to do with the "debtor's ethic." Our relationships to God and to each other need to reflect not attempts at repayment, but rather heart-felt gratitude, which can only be consummated by yet deeper relationships. As I have said before, the only way to *really* communicate to my wife how appreciative I am of her great cooking is to ask for another helping, not to say "I owe you an even better meal, and I will try to give it."

Watch out for the deadly "debtor's ethic" creeping into your life as a Christian. It will not produce, for it cannot, the freedom and joy which only Grace can give. Lift up your heart to the Lord, like the Psalmist's "cup of salvation," and happily ask the Lord for another heaping portion of Grace!

Yours, and Expecting more!

Be Encouraged!

Ask for More ... Again!

How Can I repay the Lord for all His goodness to me? I will lift up the cup of salvation and call upon the name of the Lord.
Psalm 116:12,13

Brothers and Sisters,

Let's have another helping from Psalm 116.

I want to magnify the power of Grace over the deadly "debtor's ethic." My concern is that we allow ourselves to be impacted by its incredible power.

Indeed, Grace may be the most powerful life-changing force in all the universe.

When I say that the only God-glorifying response to Grace is to "lift up the cup of salvation and call upon the name of the Lord," that is, to open your heart again to the Lord and ask for yet more Grace, I in no way intend to imply that Grace is cheap, and that it allows the receiver to carry on in sin and laziness. True Grace (as opposed to cheap, counterfeit grace) empowers and motivates. It does not excuse. Rather, it demolishes all excuses, because it enables the receiver to overcome what was once impossible to overcome.

So, here is how we "lift up the cup of salvation and call upon the Name of the Lord," that is, how we open our hearts yet again and happily ask for yet more Grace.

Imagine the following scenes with me:

"Heavenly Father! Thank you for the grace you have given me to battle for holiness of heart and life. Thank you for helping me to hate sin of late and love what is good. I bless You for convicting me of sin and then empowering me

---

84

to repent. But Lord! The battle is still raging in my heart and life!

I really want to be more like Jesus.

I lift my heart to You, the One who has already given me so much Grace for the battle, and I in faith and expectation ask for more!"

Or:

"Lord, I bless you for all the power you have given me lately to be a servant in my marriage (or school, or workplace, etc.). You know how tough it has been sometimes, yet by your Grace I have had so many victories of late!

Lord! I open my heart to you, and I ask you for more Grace to serve, especially when what I really want is to be served.

Thank you Lord! I bless You for it in anticipation of it!"

Or, perhaps the following situation:

"Lord Jesus, You alone know the challenges I am facing in my life. You alone know my fightings and fears. How often I have wanted to give up! But Lord Jesus! My soul clings to You! You have been and are my strength and my shield! It is Your Grace and nothing else which has given me power to keep going.

But Lord, yesterday's power is all used up ... I lift up my heart to You yet again. I bless You that You have not tired of my continual coming.

I need Grace for today, or I will not make it. I ask You for Grace again, knowing that You are not in short supply of goodness towards those who cry out to You.

I can and will face today because of Your Grace which awaits me!"

True Grace is God's unmerited favour poured out liberally upon God's undeserving children.

Grace:

*Forgives our *past,* empowers our *present,* and secures our *future*

*Knows nothing of *laziness*

*Grace rejects any notion of *worldliness*

*Refuses to embrace *selfishness*

Grace:

*Empowers for *battle*

*Motivates for *service*

*Causes one to *hate evil and love goodness*

Grace:

*Arouses *sorrow for sin*

*Enables *repentance toward Christ*

*Assures one of *forgiveness from Christ*

There is nothing sloppy or soft about Grace. It is God's strong gift that always seeks the lowest place and there works for God's Glory and our good. There is a river of it flowing your way. But be warned! It will sweep you up in the current of God's love and purpose that will not allow you to remain worldly, lukewarm, unholy, and selfish. It will call you, and then empower you, leaving you without any excuses for your half- heartedness or your sin.

If this is the Grace that you want, then be warmly invited to "lift up the cup of salvation and call on the Name of the Lord" ... yet again ... Whatever your situation, you will not be denied. Jesus is at His *best* when we are at our *worst*.

Indeed, the only right response to Grace is to ask for more. In asking you will *never* weary the Lord Jesus. Rather, you will actually bless Him and honour Him. For:

From the fullness of His grace we have all received one blessing after another. (John 1:16)

Yours, with his plate lifted – again.

Be Encouraged!

You have Been Three Times Delivered

For You, O Lord have delivered My soul from death, My eyes from tears, and my feet from stumbling.
Psalm 116:8

Friends,

I have been feeding of late on Psalm 116. Often, during my quiet times, I stay on one small portion of the Word of God for days, or weeks, and just feast upon it. I want to encourage your hearts with the above verse, which has been such a source of encouragement to me of late.

There are three great deliverances the Psalmist praises God for in the Psalm. Let's take a look at each one of them, that our own souls may be edified.

1) A deliverance from **SIN**: For You, O Lord have delivered my soul from death ...

The Word of God tells us plainly that the "wages of sin is death" (Romans 6:23), and that the "soul that sins shall die" (Ezekiel 18:1). Here the Psalmist is extolling the Lord for delivering his soul from *death*, which must mean that the Lord has delivered his soul from *sin.*

What a great deliverance is the deliverance from sin! Oh if only we had a clearer vision of the *gravity* of our sins before a Holy God, and the wonder of forgiveness which has been secured by that Holy God through the blood of His Son!

Take a moment and thank the Lord for delivering your soul from sin and death. Lift your heart towards heaven and ask Him to reveal to you, in a deeper way, the wonder of the forgiveness of sins through Jesus.

2) A deliverance from **SADNESS:** For You, O Lord have delivered … my eyes from tears ...

Oh what sadness accompanies sin! The two are first cousins! But with the deliverance from sin, there can come a deliverance from sadness. For this same Jesus, who was a "man of sorrows and familiar with sufferings" (Isaiah 53:3), not only "took up our infirmities." but "carried our sorrows" (Isaiah 53:4).

And more, this same Jesus, who, from His Father was anointed with "the oil of joy"(Hebrews 1:9), wills that His "joy may be in us," and that our "joy may be complete" (John 15:11). Imagine this! None other than Jesus Himself, wants the *very Joy* that His Father has given *Him* to be *complete in us*!

You cannot get it clearer or better than that. Believe God for deliverance from sadness, and pursue Him for it. God wills nothing less than His Joy for each and every one of His Blood-washed children.

3) A deliverance from **STUPIDITY:** For You, O Lord have delivered … my feet from stumbling.

What folly and foolishness follows in the wake of sin! Sin leads to bad decisions, to poor choices, and takes us down dark pathways where stumbling, falling, and sadness are our sure destiny.

Yet God, the same God who delivers from sin and sadness, would deliver us from stupidity by making us wise in His ways. He has given us His Word to make us "wise for salvation." (2 Timothy 3:15) He loves to give wisdom - generously - to all who ask Him. (James 1:5)

Why settle for a life of folly when you can live in wisdom? We do not have to stumble through life making one foolish move after another. The Lord is happy to make us wise, and to place our feet upon level places.

Open yourself to God's Word. Raise your heart towards heaven and ask the Lord to impart His wisdom to you, delivering you from foolishness. Hide God's Word in your heart (Psalm 119:11), and believe that it will deliver your feet from stumbling.

So I leave you with these three great deliverances. I pray that they will be a sure part of your experience in Christ.

Yours, delivered, delivered, delivered!

Be Encouraged!

The Lord is Worth Your Best

But you ask, 'How have we shown contempt for your name?'
Malachi 1:6

Beloved in Christ,

I want to kick things off with a question:

What is Jesus Christ worth to you?

Now, that question may sound a bit obvious to you, but it truly is a question of great value, one deserving of true consideration and an honest answer.

As you ponder your answer, I want to take you back with me to the little book of Malachi, the last book of the Old Testament, written to God's Israel some 400 years before the time of Christ.

God spoke through the prophet of his concern for His honour. His people were defiling their worship in the offering of their "cast-offs" to Him. It was not that they did not believe in Him, but, worse, it was that in believing, they had little regard for Him. He was not *worth* much to them. Their gifts and offering represented not their best, but their left-overs. Having reserved the best for themselves, they felt it right that the God of Eternity, who had redeemed and preserved them, be served with their blemished remnants. Hear just a few of God's words to his Israel spoken through Malachi:

You show contempt for my Name ... You place defiled food on my altar.

When you bring blind, crippled, or diseased animals for sacrifice, is that not wrong? Try offering that to your governor. Would he be pleased with you?

Cursed is the cheat who has an acceptable male in his flock, and vows to give it, but then sacrifices a blemished animal to the Lord.

Oh that one of you would shut the temple doors! ... I am not pleased with you.

In Malachi's day, God's people were no longer offering their best to Him, thereby showing contempt for their God. God was not pleased, and actually desired that someone would shut the whole thing down and close the Temple!

Now, let's let this background speak to us as we get back to answering our question:

What is Jesus Christ worth to you?

The very heart of "worship" means to ascribe "worth-ship" to the Lord. And such ascribing of "worth-ship" of necessity *must* involve the giving of our very best to the Lord. We cannot serve Him with our:

Cast-offs, Spare-change

Left-overs, Fag-ends

Now, God is not hard to please. He receives us in grace, loves us in grace, and keeps us in grace. But we mistake grace, and cheapen it, when we wrongly believe that grace gives license for laziness and deliberate second best. We, like Israel of old, dishonour the Lord to his face, and before the watching world.

Wonder with me:

Should a pub be better cared for than a church?

Should our hobbies come first and the Lord's work last?

Should we keep our satellite dish at the expense of our tithe?

Brothers and sisters, let us consider the immeasurable value of our Lord Jesus Christ. We say that He is the most wonderful and beautiful Being in all the Universe, but let us demonstrate that to be true in the giving of the very best of ourselves and our substance to Him.

May we open and lift our hearts to the Lord, asking Him and trusting Him for grace to give Him our utmost this year.

Yours for the sake of the Best.

Be Encouraged!

Burning Hearts Beat Burning Books

...that we may live peaceful and quiet lives in all godliness and holiness [for] this is good, and pleases God our Saviour who wants all men to be saved and to come to a knowledge of the truth.
1 Timothy 2:2-4

Dear Pilgrim,

Some years ago, on the 9th anniversary of the "9/11" terror-tragedies, The Dove World Outreach Center (a congregation of about 50 people), was planning a "Koran Burning" ceremony. If you visited their website, you would have found articles such as "Ten Reasons to Burn a Koran."

As a pastor I felt a need to respond to this.

First, let me say unequivocally, that I do not hold the Koran to be a book inspired by God, bringing to the world a true message of salvation. I believe Islam to be a religion which has a very different view of God, man, sin, and salvation from that which we find in the Bible. I believe that Muslims need Jesus just as surely as I do. Acts 4:12, "Salvation is found in no one else, for there is no other name under heaven given to men by which we must be saved," applies to all peoples.

Moreover, the Koran paves the way for a religion in which warfare and militancy are intrinsic, and for which violence is not an aberration (as it is in Christianity,) but actually consistent with the life and practice of its founder.

So, is it right for Christians to burn the Koran, or, for that matter, the holy book of any other religious group? Is the Dove World Outreach Center displaying authentic Christian witness in their proposed Koran Burning?

———

94

No, it is not right for Christians to burn Korans, and no, our Christian brothers at DWOC are not displaying authentic Christian witness with such action. The instance in Ephesus in Acts 19 where there was a book burning took place as idolaters turned to Christ, and in repentance, destroyed the tools of their previous idolatry. As such it has no bearing upon this current situation. (If a converted Muslim feels the need to burn his old Koran that is his business.)

Let me give three reasons why I would want to distance ourselves from such activity:

1) It is beneath the dignity of Jesus Christ. He who is the Image of the Invisible God, the Eternal Son of the Eternal Father, does not need His followers to employ the tactics of the world in order to witness to the world. Let Nazis burn books. Let Muslims bomb churches. Jesus Christ has commanded us to "love our enemies." Indeed, "the weapons of our warfare are not the weapons of the world. On the contrary, they have divine power to demolish strongholds" (2 Corinthians 10:4). Burning Korans is worldly and therefore weak. Proclaiming the gospel in the face of opposition, praying for those who hate you, and serving those who would and might kill you is Heavenly and presents a power the world cannot know.

2) The Christian Gospel allows and encourages the free exchange of ideas and does not need any form of a thought clamp-down. Whenever the Apostle Paul would enter a city, be it ever so pagan, he would seek out the places of learning and worship and dialogue and debate. Perhaps his detractors tried to silence him, stone him, hound him out of town, or kill him, but he and his colleagues doggedly pressed on, presenting the message of One Crucified and Risen, and trusted that message to be "the power of God unto salvation." The Gospel can hold its own in the marketplace of ideas, and does not need brutish tactics. Koran burning is cheap and requires a low-level of disciplined thought. Rather invite your Muslim neighbour over for dinner (avoid the pork!), and invite him

to *bring his* book, engaging in a vivid exchange of ideas as you open *your* Book in a vigorous (Spirit empowered) after-dinner dialogue! Jesus will acquit himself "just fine" in such a situation ... Koran burning will only serve to stifle the genuine exchange of ideas and true Christian witness.

3) Koran burning engages a worldly spirit which can only lead to other forms of violent reprisals. We see absolutely nothing of this in the New Testament, where such violence was never instigated by the followers of Jesus. Shall we then move on to Mosque burning? Perhaps our Muslim neighbours will now feel justified in a spree of Church bombing. This is contrary to the express will of God in the New Testament, where we are encouraged to pray for:

... kings and all those in authority, that we may live peaceful and quiet lives in all godliness and holiness [for] this is good, and pleases God our Saviour who wants all men to be saved and to come to a knowledge of the truth. (1 Timothy 2:2-4).

For these reasons at least, I distance myself from the spirit and actions of The Dove World Outreach Center. It is easier to set a book on fire than to set your heart on fire. Join me in praying that these folks, and those like them, will repent of their base intentions and seek a burning heart for the lost, rather than simply burning the sacred book of the lost.

May we be aggressive in Love, certain of the uniqueness of the Lord Jesus in a mixed up world, ready to live and die for Him who alone is all Grace and Truth.

I'll take a heart that burns for Jesus over a Koran burning any day!

Yours for Christ Alone,.

Be Encouraged!

God is Not Like Us

Do not pray for this people nor offer any plea or petition for them, because I will not listen when they call to me in the time of their distress.
Jeremiah 11:14

Brothers and Sisters,

I want you to consider the weight of the above word from the Lord to His People Israel through His prophet Jeremiah.

There is a sense in which we should stand aghast in the presence of such a word. How can the Covenant God of Israel actually tell His prophet that He will no longer listen to any prayers offered to Him by His own People?

What does this say about the Israel of God? More importantly, what does this say about The God of Israel?

Israel had become too casual in regards to God. They had lost a sense of His utter Holiness. They had made themselves familiar with a whole host of other "gods," the idols of the peoples around them. God had said to them:

You have as many gods as you do towns, O Judah; and the altars you have set up to that shameful god Baal are as many as the streets of Jerusalem. (11:13)

Now, by our modern notions, we really cannot see the problem. OK, Israel should not pray to other gods, and burning incense to Baal is not "best practice," but what is the "big deal?" Our modern denim-wearing "god" may faintly wish that His people would not wander from Him, but he certainly does not have the guts to *do anything* about it, does He? Besides, isn't our "chilled out" deity too cool to really care? What's a bit of idolatry in the grand scheme of things (by which we mean, *our* personal peace, fun, and prosperity)?

97

God's Israel had lost sight of Israel's God. They had forgotten that He exists for His own Glory and cannot share His Glory with another. They had forgotten that they were jealously His, that He had called them, cleansed them, delivered them, preserved them to be His Precious People, a witness and a blessing to the entire world. Perhaps they had come to see Him as essentially like them, but a bit bigger. Perhaps they had become enamored with the nations around them, and their gods which promised wealth and fun and demanded little in terms of separation and holiness.

Perhaps we have become like them.

Now, the "chilled out" god, the one who puts his feet on the chair, the "buddy upstairs," the one to whom it matters little how his people think and act and worship and speak, would have no problem with a wandering-hearted Israel, or with our wandering hearts.

BUT ... Such a god ...

Does not exist. Not anywhere in the universe. He is a figment of carnal imaginations.

Regarding such deliberately carnal people, the Holy One says: "Don't even pray for them." Now this means that they have gone way down the path of idolatry and carnality. They have been ignoring warnings and taking blessings for granted for a long time.

But just *think* about what this tells us of God's character. He simply is not the pushover we sometimes think Him to be. He can get tough when He must. His grace cannot be cheapened by our love of the world and our desire to have a mascot and servant rather than a Saviour and Lord. If we push Him too far, He who is "slow to anger and abounding in love" is fully capable of saying "I, at least for a time, am going to withdraw - not my Eternal Covenant - but my nearness, protection, daily kindness, close provision, and joy-giving." He will leave us to our idols, to our false gods, each of whom will in the short-term thrill, but in the long-term prove themselves to be cruel and deceptive.

His admonition to Jeremiah to not even pray for His People was not God going back on His covenant, but an expression of Him keeping it. He willed their holiness and their fullness. He willed them to be a unique nation, and a clear witness. Their compromised hearts and lives were muddying their testimony and would eventually lead to their destruction. This was an act of discipline of the severest sort. Temporary abandonment to their own wicked designs was for the sake of full restoration to purpose and blessing.

We learn that our God is faithful to us no matter what it may cost us. The people of Israel wanted a Faithful God, and got one ... but this faithfulness made discipline necessary. You want a Faithful God? There is one - but only one - available. He will draw you into His covenant of Love and this will mean that He will love you with purpose and determination, for His Glory and for your good, even if He has to get tough.

I think we need a new understanding of the "One with whom we have to do."

Therefore, let us be thankful ... and so worship God acceptably with reverence and awe. For our God is a consuming fire. (Hebrews 12:28-29)

May the True God Grant Us Grace and Peace to Pursue Him in Holiness .

Yours, with trembling.

Be Encouraged!

Jesus Will Give You Grace For The Race

Let us run with perseverance the race marked out for us. Let us fix our eyes on Jesus, the Author and Perfecter of our faith, who for the joy set before Him endured the cross, scorning its shame, and sat down at the right hand of God. Consider Him, who endured such opposition from sinful men, so that you will not grow weary and lose heart.
Hebrews 12:1-3

Beloved,

I love stories of human endeavour and accomplishment.

I have a new hero.

I want to take you back to 1968, and the Mexico City Olympics. It is the Marathon race ... the winner, Mamo Waldi of Ethiopia has been declared, and his celebrations have begun.

It is now 7pm. The race has been over for more than an hour.

The sun has set.

Many have left the stadium as the cold evening air settles upon the high-altitude city.

But the race is not over. There is still one man left to enter the stadium.

John Stephen Akhwari, from Tanzania, is still out running, hobbling, walking, through the city streets. (I recently saw a film of his wobbly entrance ... it made me weep with joy and conviction!)

He has fallen badly and severely cut his right knee. He is bloodied and bandaged. Every bone in his body is aching. His energy is spent.

No one would blame him for quitting. Everyone would understand. Seventeen other runners have quit. ...

John Stephen Akhwari refuses to give up.

As he enters the stadium, slowed to a hobbling walk, the remaining fans begin to cheer him on. They rise to their feet as he summons the very last ounces of energy from deep within and begins to run his last lap.

To a standing ovation, John Stephen Akhwari finishes the 1968 Olympic Marathon long after the other competitors have showered and changed. He is perhaps the most applauded last place finisher in history.

Following the race, this is what my new hero said:

My country did not send me 5000 miles to Mexico City to start the race. They sent me 5000 miles to finish the race.

Now, he has not gone down in history among the great names like Paula Radcliff or Usain Bolt. You most likely have not heard of him.

He never won a major competition. But he is a winner in other categories.And he is a real inspiration to me in my quest to follow my Lord Jesus Christ to the end.

Beloved in Christ, Jesus did not save us just so that we could make a start and then give it up when things get a bit tough, or even real tough. He saved us to finish, to cross the line.

The same Lord who said, "He who endures to the end shall be saved" is the Saviour who promises, "I will never leave you or forsake you."

He promises us grace to run this race.

He gives strength to the weary.

He promises to be with us until the end. Then, LIFE BEGINS!

Let's take inspiration from our Tanzanian runner ... And then fix our eyes firmly upon our Saviour and run the race marked out before us!

Grace to You!

Be Encouraged!

God Will Give You The Heart He Wants You To Have

Teach me your way, O Lord, and I will walk in your Truth. Give me an undivided heart That I may fear your Name.
Psalm 86:11

Beloved in Christ,

Do you ever wonder what or how or if you should pray for yourself? Great wisdom can be gained by reading the Psalms and discovering what the Psalmist prayed in regards to himself.

We can be certain that we are praying in the will of God when we pray the very prayers that the inspired writers of the Bible prayed.

In the passage quoted at the top of this letter, David is bringing his heart before the Lord. The passage is rich in instruction for us. The core of his prayer is found in the words:

Give me an undivided heart.

Clearly David, a man of God, is aware of a *divided* heart, or he would not be asking the Lord for an *undivided* heart. This tips us off that the first step towards an undivided heart is recognizing and admitting to the Lord that you don't have one!

What does a divided heart look and act like? I do not have to look far to find and research a divided heart. My investigation needs go no farther than my own breast.

A divided heart loves God sometimes and the world other times. It sometimes denies self, and at other times it serves self. One moment it hates sin; at another moment it finds sin almost irresistibly attractive. A divided heart is inconsistent. It can love others one day, and be full of malice on another. It can be warm and worshipful, or cold and carnal. A divided heart cannot know a steady stream of joy, but only joy in spurts.

According to David, the key attribute of a divided heart is that it does not fear God. By this David does not mean a craven, destructive fear, but a reverent, awestruck attitude towards the Lord in worship and lifestyle, earnestly and happily shunning the ugliness of sin and evil in preference to the beauty of God in His holiness. A heart which fears the Lord sees the Lord as a Holy Judge, and takes His saving mercy to itself in deepest gratitude. A divided heart cannot experience this "fear of the Lord."

A divided heart is a complicated thing. It is miserable, inconsistent, untrustworthy, ungrateful, and foolishly fearless.

David, this worshipping man who had known both the beauty of holiness and the ugliness of sin, saw such a heart in himself. I see one in myself. David prayed and asked the Lord to give him a simple, undivided heart.

Such a prayer is proof of the work of grace in his life. Even the *desire* for an undivided heart is impossible without the influence of the grace of God upon a divided heart. "Lord! When I look inside, I don't like what I see! I ask You, Lord of all Grace and Goodness, to do a work in my heart and make it what it is not naturally! Give me (for I cannot produce it myself) a heart that is wholly Yours."

I believe that an undivided heart is possible, or the inspired David would not have prayed for one. I believe by the grace of God one can have a heart that is simple, reverent, and solely the property of the Lord.

It is possible because the Lord is happy to give it.

I don't know what you are praying for in terms of yourself, but you cannot do better than David did in asking God to do open-heart surgery, and as the King James Bible puts it, "unite" his heart. For, an undivided, united heart will see everything that comes its way in a new light, and all of life will take on a new perspective.

104

I cannot echo the Psalmist's prayer better than the words of Charles Wesley, and I leave them with you to meditate upon and pray for yourself.

> O for a heart to praise my God,
> a heart from sin set free,
> a heart that always feels thy blood
> so freely shed for me.
>
> A heart resigned, submissive, meek,
> my great Redeemer's throne,
> where only Christ is heard to speak,
> where Jesus reigns alone.
>
> A humble, lowly, contrite heart,
> believing, true, and clean,
> which neither life nor death can part
> from Christ who dwells within.
>
> A heart in every thought renewed
> and full of love divine,
> perfect and right and pure and good,
> a copy, Lord, of Thine.
>
> Thy nature, gracious Lord, impart;
> come quickly from above;
> write thy new name upon my heart,
> thy new, best name of Love.

Yours, and wanting All My Heart For Jesus,

Be Encouraged!

God At Work In You For Your Good

Therefore, since we are receiving a Kingdom that cannot be shaken, let us be thankful, and worship God acceptably with reverence and awe. For our "God is a consuming fire."
Hebrews 12:28,29

Dear Miracle Project,

God is not nice! I think of the question asked of Aslan, C.S. Lewis' Lion in the *Narnia* series:

"Is He *safe*?"

"No, but He is *good*."

Likewise, our God is not *Nice*. He is too loving, too holy, too terrible (I use the word here in the old-fashioned sense) to be "nice".

"Nice" is a weak word. God is not weak. A cup of tea can be "nice."

A "nice" God would never really care about developing souls for a Holy Habitation in Heaven.

A "nice" God would be really only concerned that we all have a jolly good time. Our character would be of little interest to Him.

A "nice" God would shrug His shoulders at our sins and sheepishly look the other way.

A "nice" God would never have a hell. A "nice" God would never be feared. He would not want to be. He would not be worthy of worship and could never really be trusted.

God is *not* nice. And for this we can and shall be eternally grateful.Consider with me the following Scriptures. Take some time and meditate on what they have to teach us about what God is like:

Therefore, since we are receiving a Kingdom that cannot be shaken, let us be thankful, and worship God acceptably with reverence and awe. For our God is a consuming fire. (Hebrews 12:28,29)

.... now, for a little while you may have to suffer grief in all kinds of trials. These have come so that your faith - of greater worth than gold, which perishes even though refined by fire - may prove genuine and may result in praise glory and honour when Jesus Christ is revealed. (1 Peter 1:6-7)

God disciplines us for our good, that we might share in his holiness.(Hebrews 12: 10)

Think about what we have just read. Here is a God who is a "consuming fire," sending painful trials that we may have a purer faith, disciplining us that we may share in His holiness.

Hardly a "nice" God.

What is clear is that God has a different agenda than most of us. Therefore, unless we get on board with His agenda and tear up our own, we are going to either have to invent some soppy idol that suits our scant idea of what "god" should be, or we are going to forever be limping from one sort of faith crisis to another. Those of us who really just want to be "left alone," forever in search of the path of least resistance and a "nice" life, had better leave real Christianity off altogether.

The real God, the one that the Bible reveals, is fitting our souls for His Heaven, and this means tearing us away from our hell-bound selves. This is a monumental task, which involves no less that the death of His Son, the ongoing ministry of His Word and His Spirit, the purifying heat of trials and tribulations, and, often, not a small amount of pain.

It is as though over every true twice-born child of Grace the words: "Danger! God At Work!" have been inscribed. To paraphrase C.S. Lewis: "You asked for a God of Love ... Well, you have one."

The day will come when those who have been transformed by this Loving God will "see Him face to face," " as He is." On that day, His Joy "will be complete in us" and true, Resurrection Life will begin. We need to see His Divine demolition of our old selves and His rebuilding of us into our New Selves in light of His glorious eternal purposes for us.

So, make yourself a nice cup of tea, open your Bible, and get before your Loving God and ask Him to do His work in your life.

Yours, For His Glory and your good.

Be Encouraged!

You Will Never Exhaust God's Super-Abundant Grace

*From the fullness of His grace we have all received one
blessing after another.*
John1:16

Dear Family in Christ,

As I greet you in the matchless Name of Jesus Christ, my desire is
that we refresh our souls together with the verse above.

I am increasingly amazed at the goodness of the Lord
towards us, who, deserving only wrath, are receiving "one blessing
after another."

The verse at the top of this letter, found in the prologue of
John's Gospel, is brimming over with promise and encouragement
for the earnest follower of Jesus. We can perhaps best discover the
riches of what it says by considering what it *does not* say.

*It *does not* say: "From His grace we have all received one
blessing."

Now, if it did just say that, it would still be truly remarkable
when we consider that we do not naturally deserve *any* blessing.
What we *deserve* is just punishment for sin. If God, in His grace,
gave us *one* good thing, that would be an act of immeasurable
kindness on the part of Him who owes us nothing but judgment.

*It *does not* say: "From the fullness of His grace *some* have
received ..."

That is how we would do it. We would give *some* "one
blessing after another," but to the rest we would just give one
blessing, perhaps two or three, or maybe none at all. We would

---

109

determine on merit who "deserved" blessings, and give accordingly. Upon inspection, we see that blessings based upon merit would not be grace at all.

*It *does not* say: "From the *limited reserve* of His grace we have received ..."

Most of us view God's reservoir of grace as bounded. Perhaps a fairly large lake for some, perhaps a mere puddle of grace in the minds of others, but in any case, limited and therefore needing to be rationed. To such minds, grace can be exhausted as God gets exasperated with our endless needs.

Look again at what the verse *says* about the Grace of God revealed in Jesus Christ:

From The fullness of His grace we have all received one blessing after another.

We are told here of a *boundless* sea of undeserved favour and strength available for the *ordinary believer.* The King James Version translates the verse like this:

And of His fullness we have all received, and grace for grace.

I love this translation because it roots the wellspring of available grace directly in the very Person of Jesus: "And of His fullness." Certainly this then is an infinite pool of grace for the believer.

This is overwhelmingly good news when we consider that Christ is calling us each to the supernatural life of discipleship. We are being called to the *impossible.* We must be either divinely resourced, or we will fail from the start.

Consider the call of Christ:

"Deny yourself, take up your cross, and follow Me."

"Love your enemies and pray for those who use you."

"Crucify your sinful nature."

"Consider yourself dead to sin but alive to God."

"Husbands, love your wives."

"Wives, respect your husbands."

"Fix your minds on things above."

"Children obey your parents."

"Go into all the world and preach the Gospel to all creation."

"Consider others better than yourselves."

"Bless those who persecute you."

"Love your neighbour as yourself."

This is clearly a *super*natural life. It is not about "self improvement" or "trying to do better." It is nothing less than the *Life of God* being lived out in *us*. It requires God's limitless resources, which are *readily available* to the simplest and weakest among us. He gives us grace to do the hard thing, the good thing, the impossible thing ... That our lives may be a reflection of Him to this world.

Peter puts it this way:

His divine power has given us everything we need for life and godliness through our knowledge of Him who has called us by His own glory and goodness. (2 Peter 1:3)

Believe this! Get into it! Lift your heart heavenward and *receive* grace for a supernatural life. It may be time for you to remove your pauper's garments, and begin to live like one for whom God in Christ is making all grace continually available. Open up your heart to Jesus, and ask Him to fill you with His very own supernatural power. Ask Him to make your life a miracle. Ask Him to take you to new places with Him, to places you never dreamed you could go. Ask him to reshape your character from the inside out, to reform you into His very likeness. Trust His grace to make you as holy as you can possibly be this side of Heaven.

In the light of His Infinite Resources, to settle for anything less is a tragedy.

Yours, believing and receiving.

Be Encouraged!

Your Life ... And Your Death ... Are Precious To God

Precious in the sight of the Lord is the
Death of His saints.
Psalm 116:15

Dearest Sisters and Brothers,

Ahh! How hard it can be to say "good-bye" to a precious brother or sister! How painful are these partings! They make us long for that Day when there will be "no more death, or mourning, or crying, or pain" as "the old order of things [will have] passed away" (Rev. 21:4).

Each time we gather to commend one of us to our Heavenly Father, He designs such moments of grief and tears to be opportunities for His Grace to work deeply in our lives. He weans us from this sad "old order" which we love and to which we cling, and causes us to look toward and long for Heaven (our destiny!), for which we have been redeemed from sin.

In the verse above, the Psalmist gives twice-born believers great comfort as they survey this landscape of death. Focus with me on that word "**precious.**" It means "valuable," "prized," "excellent," "honorable," "costly," "watched over."

Ponder this. Here we have a precious believer in Jesus. A child of grace, born of the Spirit of God. He finds himself still to be limited by death ... a limit God Himself has imposed on the entire human family, a family whose sinful inclination is to want to be "like God."

This God-imposed limit keeps a fallen race in check before a Holy God, and keeps a redeemed believer humble and hungry for Heaven. So this child of grace gets sick or suffers an accident. His days on earth are cut short. He is reminded by his own demise that he is "dust" and a "vapour." The pain in his body, the loss of strength, beauty, and mental agility tells him plainly that his glory is like the flower of the field which blooms for a little while, and then suddenly is remembered no more.

But this twice-born child of grace is destined for Eternity. He has been redeemed for a greater purpose than this fallen realm can offer. His passing into fuller purpose necessarily involves him dying. There is no way around this. The Christian must die just like the non-Christian. Death limits him too. But he dies only to gain life. And (and please get this) this believer's death is "precious in the sight of" his God and Saviour. This means that it is overseen, monitored, regarded, valued, by the Lord who shed blood for him, has prepared a place for him, and who now summons him to a higher purpose. God, who has numbered his days (see Psalm 139), is shepherding him through the "valley of the shadow of death" (Psalm 23) and into His very presence.

We who remain weep. And we should. We grieve our loss. We cry out to God in our pain, longing and wishing that He had ordained more days for our beloved. God understands this. Abraham mourned Sarah's death, Isaac Rebekah's, John the Baptist's friends mourned his death, and those who loved our Lord Jesus in His earthly life mourned His death.

But in our grief, we are being called to lift our sights. We are being called to be … *believers*. God has not been caught by surprise in these sad losses. He feels our weakness and comforts us through the Gospel in our loss, but He also summons us to a new place of trust and worship. These loses have not taken place outside of the vista of the Shepherd's watch.

Precious in the sight of the Lord is the death of His saints.

Funerals will not cease until Jesus comes back. One day, I may attend yours, or you mine. We need to have a believer's perspective on these sad days, or we will simply be despairing like those who have no hope. When we look beyond the vale of tears and focus on a Hope that will not disappoint (no believer will ever be proven a fool for putting his hope in Jesus,) we are acting like children of grace and citizens of heaven.

May the Lord Himself grant us encouragement and eternal hope.

Yours, and carefully watched over.

Be Encouraged!

God's Law of Sowing and Reaping Cannot Be Broken

Do not be deceived: God cannot be mocked. A man reaps what he sows. The one who reaps to please his sinful nature will from that nature reap destruction. The one who sows to please the Spirit, from the Spirit will reap eternal life.
Galatians 6:7,8

Saints,

Many years ago I was a young pastor in the hills of Northwest Arkansas.On a dusty dirt road lived an "old timer," named Wilbur (in Arkansas talk he was just called "Mister Wilbur"). He told me the following true story that had happened in those Arkansas hills when he was a boy.

Not far from Mister Wilbur lived another lad, on another farm tucked away in the Ozark Mountains. Mister Wilbur knew the boy. Now that boy had a bit of a mean streak in him, and he did not like one of his neighbour men very much.

As time went on, that ornery lad came up with a plan to "git [get] his neighbour but good" (as they say in Arkansas).

There is a weed that grows in Arkansas (and in much of the world) called Johnson Grass. It is deadly to cattle (it contains cyanide), and can almost never be eradicated from a field once embedded. To this day farmers will work a lifetime to get a field free of that deadly weed. Well, Mister Wilbur's nasty neighbour boy went out one day and found some Johnson Grass in full seed by the wayside. He stripped the heads of seed off the stalks and put the seeds in a satchel.

Then ... that night ... he made his dusty way to that old neighbour's place, snuck through the woods, climbed the barbed-wire fence, and entered the man's pasture. By moonlight he reached into his old satchel and scattered handfuls of Johnson Grass seed everywhere.

Having accomplished his dastardly deed he stole away through the night. The man never knew the lad had paid his pasture this troublesome visit.

Before long the seed germinated, and sure enough, that Johnson Grass grew to become a curse to the farmer and his pasture from then on.

Time passed and the lad grew into a handsome young man. As the (true) story goes, his neighbour, the very one to whom a few years before he had paid his nasty nocturnal visit, had a little girl who likewise grew into a lovely young lady.

The lad "took a shine" to her. More than that, he fell in love with her.

He married her.

As a wedding gift, the old man, gave the young man the only thing a poor mountain farmer had to give ... his land. The once naughty lad, now a fine young married man became the proud owner of ... a field full of Johnson Grass. A True Story! Just ask Mister Wilbur!

Talk about your chickens coming home to roost! What a picture of life! What a lesson!

God warns us in His Word against sowing bad seed. What we put in determines what sprouts, grows, and produces. It is the simple, and changeless law of sowing and reaping. We *cannot* outsmart this law. If we sow to please the sinful nature, we will from that nature reap destruction. It is inevitable. There is no way around it and noone can beat the odds.

God's ways are unchangeable, and neither you nor I can find a way around them.

What films do you watch?

What conversations do you hold?

What books do you read?

The Word of God counsels us to sow with wisdom and great care:

Finally, brothers, whatever is true, whatever is noble, whatever is right, whatever is pure, whatever is lovely, whatever is admirable – if anything is excellent or praiseworthy – think about such things. (Philippians 4:8)

Whoever sows to please their flesh, from the flesh will reap destruction; whoever sows to please the Spirit, from the Spirit will reap eternal life. (Galatians 6:8)

The results of our sowing are plain, permanent, and profound: Destruction or Life.

Just ask Mister Wilbur.

Yours, sowing for Life.

Be Encouraged!

You Can Dream Heavenly Dreams

Because Your love is better than life, my lips will glorify You.
Psalm 63:3

Beloved in Christ,

Someone has said that the only thing worse than unrealized dreams are realized dreams. To put it another way, there is little sadder than climbing to the top of the ladder only to realize that you have had it leaning against the wrong wall all along. Pity the man who realizes his life's goals, only to find that those very goals don't fill the yawning void in his soul. Pity the woman who builds her dream home, only to find herself trapped inside it. Pity the person whose dreams are too small.

We have been created by the Lord and for the Lord. We cannot be fulfilled in any final sense with anything short of Him. The wise soul will realize this and not expect true and deepest fulfillment out of anything here below. The wise soul will be most surely thankful for human love and earthly pleasures, but he will not dare expect to have his soul satisfied with the passing things of earth ... even the very best things that this life has to offer.

If your dreams can be fulfilled with *anything* here on earth, then your dreams are too small! A perfect marriage, a wonderful home, a dear family, financial success ... These may all be things for which we are thankful, truly thankful. But the healthy soul will never expect from them final satisfaction.

The healthy Christian soul plans on "peaking" in Heaven.

Expecting deep fulfillment from the shallow pools of temporal blessings actually destroys even the little pleasures that earthly things are capable of offering.

God designed taste and sight and touch, human love and temporal beauty to be freely enjoyed and to point us to the Eternal and Lasting. But when we drink too long at the trough of the temporary, we drink it dry, only soon to thirst again, blaming the trough for failing. We then find ourselves disappointed in the marriage, or job, or house, or meal, when in fact we were asking of it the impossible in the first place, namely, deepest satisfaction. We end up loathing the good, because from it we expected the Best.

Augustine was right when he observed that God had made us for Himself, and that we are, and will of necessity continually be, restless until we come to rest in Him. It cannot be any other way. It is a matter of design. And here is the wonderful surprise: It is when we cease drinking from the shallow, and turn instead to the deep, when we wake from our little dreams and begin to dream big dreams that require a Heaven to fulfill, that we are set free to *enjoy* what we have now. It is when I stop expecting my wife to meet my deepest need, looking instead to the Lord for such fulfillment, that my wife actually becomes *enjoyable* again. It is when I remember that Jesus is preparing a place for me in Glory, that I actually become content with the place He has given me here on earth. It is when I remember that all the purpose which the Lord has put within me will finally be fulfilled in Eternity, not here in Time, that I become content with what purpose I have now, and I enjoy my job again.

Dreams which require Heaven set the Dreamer free to live on earth. If you are dreaming little dreams, you are missing your greater purpose, and your little dreams realized may prove to be nightmares. Marriages that are being asked to thrill and satisfy forever end up in divorce courts. Jobs which are expected to give ultimate purpose and satisfaction end up giving ulcers and sleepless nights. Dream homes end up as idolatrous bottomless pits of projects and finance (indeed, the word "mortgage" is derived from the Latin for "death grip"!) You have been created for the Lord and for His Heaven, and nothing else can finally satisfy the cries of your heart.

It is therefore your duty, your happy duty, your solemn duty, to nurture your soul with the Word of God, "setting your mind on things above." That means reminding yourself over and over again that Christ alone is your fullness, and asking Him for His Joy and Life to be alive in you. You must refuse to allow your mind to become a little idol factory conjuring up little destructive dreams, and ask the Lord to give you Dreams which can - finally - only be fulfilled in His Heaven.

Content, but not satisfied ... That is the condition of the healthy Christian soul.

Sweet Dreams.

Be Encouraged!

We Are Living In the Greatest Miracle

The Word became flesh, and made His dwelling among us. We have seen his glory, the glory of the One and Only, full of grace and truth.
John 1:14

Greetings Brothers and Sisters!

If you were asked, "What is the greatest of all miracles?" what would you answer? Perhaps you would consider the feeding of the 5000, Jesus walking on water, or the raising of Lazarus to top the bill. The creation of all that there is out of nothing would no doubt rank high on any list, as would the resurrection of Jesus from the dead.

I think I agree with theologian Wayne Grudem that the Incarnation, the Eternal Jesus taking on human flesh, is the greatest of all miracles. Lets consider together the magnificence of this event:

The Apostle John, in the prologue to his monumental Gospel, begins by telling us that Jesus of Nazareth is no less than the Eternal God:

In the beginning was the Word and the Word was with God, and the Word was God. (John 1:1)

So, from the beginning we realize that when we talk about Jesus, we are not just talking about a great person, even the greatest of all persons, but about God Himself. John then tells us, emphatically, that this same Jesus is the Creator of all that there is:

Through Him all things were made; without Him nothing was made that has been made. (1:3)

But John, the simple fisherman turned profound Truth Writer, does not stop there!

In Him was Life, and that Life was the Light of men. (1:4)

So now we are to see that this carpenter from Nazareth is the source of all Life and the very answer to the cry of the human heart for meaning and purpose.

Now, if we were thinking right, our jaws would be beginning to drop by now. We would be realizing that when we're saying "We believe in Jesus," we are making the most profound confession of faith possible ...

But the Apostle does not leave us with the Eternal, Life-Giving, Creating Jesus. He takes us where no human invention would ever dare to take us. He takes us where no other belief-system (religion) dares to go:

The Word became flesh and made His dwelling among us. We have seen His glory ...

This is what Christian theologians call "The Incarnation." The hymn writer has spoken of it in poetic phrases such as

"Veiled in flesh the Godhead see. Hail the Incarnate Deity."

And:

"Our God contracted to a span, incomprehensibly made man."

It is this doctrine which separates Christianity from the religions of the world ... all of them. For "religion" at its essence is about *man* doing things to find and appease God (or the gods). Christianity is about *God* doing things. It is *God* taking the initiative. The Incarnation of God in Christ is the invasion of this rebel planet by a rescuing God. No human being would have ever thought of a God who:

"Emptied Himself of all but love, and bled for Adam's helpless race."

Jesus of Nazareth simply cannot be put in the same category as any other "great" man or woman. For in Christ we see two natures in one: Fully God and fully man. Mohammed was a human ... Period. Gandhi was a human ... Full Stop. Mother Teresa was a human ... Nothing more. Jesus was God and human, and so He is forever. As such He is both the way *up* and the way *down.* He is the way *up* for lowly man to exalted God, and the way *down* for Exalted God to lowly man. He is the mediator and the sin bearer. As the Son of God, He is the Father's Advocate towards our fallen race, and as the Son of Man, He is this fallen race's Advocate with the Father.

In Christ the Eternal, Transcendent God becomes the intimate, immanent God. In Christ the invisible God is seen:

No one has ever seen God, but God the One and Only, who is at the Father's side, has made Him known. (1:18)

Though you will never plumb the depths of the mystery of the Incarnation, take time to pause and ponder, worship and wonder at the manger. Christmas is mind-boggling. Don't even try to get your mind around the wonder of "God ... in Christ ... reconciling the world to Himself" (2 Corinthians 5:19). Just do what the Wise Men did: Bow in worship, and give Him the gift of your heart. For that is the only reasonable response.

Grace and Peace be yours in Abundance Through our Lord and Saviour Jesus Christ.

Be Encouraged!

God is After Our Stubborn Hearts

These are rebellious people, deceitful children, children unwilling to listen to the Lord's instruction. They say to the seers, "See no more visions!" and to the prophets, "Give us no more visions of what is right! Tell us pleasant things, prophesy illusions. Leave this way, get off this path, and stop confronting us with the Holy One of Israel!" Isaiah 30:9-11

Dear Child of Grace,

Now consider with me the above words from God through the prophet's pen.

Here we have the People of God, the Nation he had redeemed from Egypt by blood. Here are the very ones which He had jealously loved and chosen from all the peoples of the earth. None others had encountered Him in prophets and power. They had the Temple, the Sacrifices, the Law, the Covenants. They had been *loved* by the God of Heaven.

They were a Chosen Nation and a Royal Priesthood. They *belonged* to God Himself, in a way that no other people ever had and never would until the Church was birthed. They existed in order to declare God's praises to the whole of Adam's fallen race. *They* were *the* Nation through whom the whole of the human family would have hope in the coming of Jesus Christ.

Theirs was the Shekinah presence of God. To them belonged the day of Atonement as a remedy for sin. The Lord encamped around them. He time and again delivered them from their enemies. His mercies had been new to them every morning, and His steadfast love had never ceased.

125

Their fields were abundant, and when they strayed, His chastening hand brought them back and restored them to fullness.

There has never been a People like them ... until us.

Yet here, in Isaiah's day, we have these privileged people saying, "Stop urging us toward holiness!" "Don't warn us of judgment!" "We want nice sermonettes that leave us in our sin and make us feel good about ourselves!" "Don't place the True God before us, but give us a god that will cuddle us in our worldliness!"

Let the full shock of this come upon you. Remember just who Israel was. God's special Nation! Yet here they were stiff and hard-hearted and sin loving and worldly. Failing to treasure Yahweh above all else, they would rather have their sin than God!

So the Lord warns them through the prophet:

Because you have rejected this message ... this sin will become for you like a high wall, cracked and bulging, that collapses suddenly, in an instant. (vss 12,13)

What a warning! The prophet tells them that in rejecting the call to repentance, in stiff-arming God, their sin, the very sin that they love more than God, will be as a wall that collapses upon them ... and ruins them.

I carry something of Isaiah's concern in my heart. Not for ancient Israel, but for Jesus' Church today. When the message of holiness of heart and life becomes a burdensome message to those of us who claim to follow Jesus, when the Church grows comfortable with sin and is irritated by any who speak of repentance and genuine heart obedience, something is desperately wrong.

I find myself to be in a battle I never thought I would have to fight (I was naive). I fear that we are forgetting how to blush, that sin does not shock us any more, and that we are feeling comfortable – at home - with worldliness in our private and public lives.

We secretly love sin, so we dare not rebuke it when we find it in others, even if genuine love calls us to do so. Indeed, have we become those to whom Paul was referring who simply want teachers who will "say what their itching ears want to hear" ?(2 Tim 4:3)

Beloved, what is at stake here is Eternity. The health of souls hangs in the balance. The Gospel call is a call to die to self and follow the One the world disdains. The job of the pastor is to "cure souls" with the Gospel, and, when necessary, "confront" with the "Holy One of Israel." When the Church loses the ability to clearly discern right from wrong, sin from holiness, good behavior from bad, it is only a matter of time before collapse is inevitable.

Those of us who have been redeemed from sin by the precious blood of Jesus are the most privileged of people. As such, our treasure is Christ, and no price is too great if it means we gain Heaven and lose Hell.

May the Lord have mercy upon us in granting us tender consciences, hearts for holiness, and a true hatred of sin in its every form. May He love us enough to confront us with Himself, that we may be eager repenters, and happy followers of Jesus.

Yours, but trembling.

Be Encouraged!

God Has Called You To Be A Soldier

Endure hardship ... like a good soldier of Jesus Christ.
2Timothy2:3

Dear Church,

Should we find it remarkable that the Apostle Paul uses soldiering as a picture of the Christian's life? Perhaps in today's climate the picture of the Christian life being likened to a soldier under command and ready for battle *seems* remarkable, but it should not.

I suppose most modern, Western Christians would sooner imagine:

"Enjoy a shopping-spree life as a happy follower of Jesus!"

Or:

"Make sure that you get what you want from life! Jesus will help you!"

Or:

"Seek pleasure because Jesus came to make your dreams come true!"

Or:

"Jesus is the spice of Life! Give Him a go and see what happens!"

The problem is that many of us live in an ever-shrinking universe with Self at the centre. We view life as all about us. Life is a play, and we are on centre stage. We are bombarded from without and within with the message that it is all about "me," and therefore, *everything* including the very God of the Universe is finally here to serve *my* interests.

This misery-producing view of life has infiltrated modern Christianity. Jesus is now here to serve our wishes. He is here to answer our prayers and make our dreams come true. He will even guarantee us health and wealth if we just say the right words and keep up a positive attitude. We now occupy the centre place, and Jesus is in our orbit, here to meet our every selfish need. History is no longer about Him and his Glory, but about us and our fulfillment. The Bible is no longer a Book about God and His purposes, but a book of spells that we can use to get what we want. Salvation is no longer about God saving ruined sinners to live for His Glory no matter the cost, but about Jesus helping us to get over our problems, so that we can live our dreams.

Against such a polluted stream, the true Christian must swim. He is aware of a soldierly call. He hears his Master's voice. He realizes that life is brief, death is certain, Hell is real, and Heaven is to be his treasured goal. He listens and obeys the call of Christ to die to self, to take up the Cross (an instrument of death, not a piece of jewelry) everyday. He fears his Commanding Officer far more than he fears his enemy, and he would rather die than desert. There is the joy of an unseen world in his heart, a glimpse of Eternity in his eyes, and the satisfaction in his soul that he is indeed living for a purpose far greater than himself. His great fear is not death, but sin, and holiness is his joyful pursuit.

Whatever hardships come his way, he realizes that he is a soldier of Jesus Christ, and, not being surprised by such, he focuses upon his Commander, his sole aim being his Commander's pleasure.

Brothers and Sisters, may we be genuine Soldiers of the Lord Jesus Christ in these days of suffocating ease and complacency. May our heroes be the David Livingstons, the Hudson Taylors, the Amy Carmichaels of this world, not the Homer Simpsons and James Bonds.

Yours for Soldierly Purpose.

Be Encouraged!

God Stands Above the Waves and Storms of Life

From the ends of the earth I cry unto Thee, when my heart is overwhelmed, lead me to the rock that is higher than I.
Psalm 61:2 KJV

Dear Precious Saint,

Have you ever felt your heart to be "overwhelmed" (literally: "turned upside down")?

Have you ever felt yourself to be at the "end of the earth" (meaning: "no place left to go")?

Such are common experiences for faithful followers of Jesus this side of Heaven.

It is not unusual to find yourself feeling as though you have nowhere left to go, or as though the trials of life have completely swept over you.

*Perhaps it is a rebellious child that has turned your heart to water.

*Or perhaps marital distress has left you feeling as though you have been punched in the stomach.

*Your job may leave you with a sense of desperate hopelessness ... with no way out.

*Maybe you or your loved one has failing health, and it is all that you can do just to maintain the very basics of a functioning life.

*Aging parents may leave your emotions in tatters as you seek to love them, but they make it seem as though you can never do enough.

In Psalm 61, the psalmist was finding himself at the "ends of the earth" (just sit and consider what his feelings were like at that point). His heart was"overwhelmed" (imagine him lying down, rising, pacing, groaning). But the Psalmist gives us great instruction, right from his own experience:

From the ends of the earth I cry unto Thee ... [and here is what he cries]: *Lead me to the Rock which is higher than I ...*

In my mind I view the writer clinging to a rocky out-crop on a storm tossed sea. The waves are breaking over him, and he has nowhere to go. Life is like that sometimes! I understand what he is going through, and I am greatly encouraged by his response to his predicament ...

... He cries out to God, imploring the Lord to lead him to a place of safety from the overwhelming storm: "A Rock that is Higher than I."

Now whenever I see the word "Rock" in the Old Testament, I think that I am being fair to the Bible to think of Jesus! (See 1 Peter 2:8; 1 Cor 10:4; Romans 9:33) So, I think that through my New Testament "glasses" I can read the Psalmist's cry like this:

When I have no place left to go, and I am being swamped by life, God, Father! lead me to Jesus!

If our impossibilities cause us to cry out to our Heavenly Father, and we cry to Him to lead us to Jesus (the Higher Rock) then we can actually be removed to safety and security in Christ ... If not through the literal change in our circumstances (which our Heavenly Father *may* cause to happen), then certainly in our souls where the storm may be raging.

Beloved: You and I have a sure place to go when we are at the very end of ourselves, and life's circumstances have engulfed us. We have a "Rock that is Higher" than ourselves and our circumstances.

May the Lord Himself give us grace to cry to Him in our distresses, that we might find deliverance from Him. I leave you to meditate on the words of William Cowper:

> God moves in a mysterious way His wonders to perform; He plants His footsteps in the sea and rides upon the storm.
>
> Deep in unfathomable mines Of never failing skill, He treasures up His bright designs and works His sovereign will.
>
> Ye fearful saints, fresh courage take; The clouds ye so much dread are big with mercy and shall break in blessings on your head.
>
> Judge not the Lord by feeble sense, but trust Him for His grace; Behind a frowning providence He hides a smiling face.
>
> His purposes will ripen fast, unfolding every hour; The bud may have a bitter taste, but sweet will be the flower.
>
> Blind unbelief is sure to err and scan His work in vain; God is His own interpreter, and He will make it plain.

Grace and peace in Jesus, our Rock.

Be Encouraged!

Consecrate Your Brief Life For Eternal Purpose

Redeeming the time, because the days are evil.
Ephesians 5:16

I am becoming increasingly aware of just how fast life is whizzing by. I managed to hit 59 years this week. That means, if God grants me 70 years, and I assign each decade of my life a day of the week, I am currently on my Saturday afternoon, with the end coming Sunday at midnight ... just hours away ...

Job said it well when he said that his days flew by more swiftly than a weaver's shuttle.

Yet the key is not *duration* but *donation.* It is not about how *long*, but how *well* one lives.

The poet said it well:

> *Only one life, will soon be past. Only what's done for Christ will last;*
>
> *And when I am dying, how glad I shall beIf the Lamp of my life has burned bright for Thee.*

The Bible sobers us with the reality of just how short life is. It reminds us that life is like the flower of the field ... blooming for a moment and then withering away. It tells us that life is like a mist which appears in the morning and then vanishes. But it also entices us with the glorious hope of Heaven: We have actually been built to last! Our warranty is as long as Eternity itself!

It is those who live this brief life in view of Eternity that live it the best. It is those who hear the clock ticking, face their own demise, and live with a sense of urgency, who make the most of their pilgrimage here on Earth. I am aware of one fine Christian leader who schedules out every 15 minutes of his life, committed to not let a moment drop. We may not all be able to be so disciplined, but surely we can all answer the call of the clock, the voice of the grave, and the coming of a day of reckoning, and apply more diligence to our brief lives.

Life is too precious to waste, and Time is flying by. Take your life in hand today and re-consecrate yourself to live your days for Him. Charles Wesley said it better than I:

> Give me the faith which can remove
> And sink the mountain to a plain;
> Give me the childlike praying love,
> Which longs to build thy house again;
> Thy love, let it my heart o'er-power,
> And all my simple soul devour.
>
> I would the precious time redeem,
> And longer live for this alone,
> To spend and to be spent for them
> Who have not yet my Savior known;
> Fully on these my mission prove,
> And only breathe, to breathe thy love.
>
> My talents, gifts, and graces, Lord,
> Into thy blessed hands receive;
> And let me live to preach thy word,
> And let me to thy glory live;
> My every sacred moment spend
> In publishing the sinners' Friend.
>
> Enlarge, inflame, and fill my heart
> With boundless charity divine,
> So shall I all my strength exert,
> And love them with a zeal like thine,
> And lead them to thy open side,
> The sheep for whom the Shepherd died.

Yours, briefly in Time, But for Eternity.

Be Encouraged!

There is Hope on a Bad Day

*But if we walk in the light, as he is in the light, we have
fellowship with one another, and the blood of Jesus, his Son,
purifies us from all sin.*
1 John 1:7

Friends,

The other day I had a spiritual meltdown. It seemed to come right
out of the blue.

The day started off seeming O K. I had a time with Jesus and
was thankful for some precious things I found in His Word.

But soon thereafter I got really angry (I mean *really* angry) at
our dog ... and everything began to unravel from there.

My inner mood just got worse and worse, and I found myself
by lunchtime with my feet stuck fast in the "slough of despond." By
the end of the day I felt like Elijah under the broom tree, just wishing
that the Lord would take me on to Heaven! My dear wife could not
have been sweeter to me. I really was not too nasty to her, as it was
in my inner self that the meltdown was occurring. Nevertheless
"ash" from the meltdown fell upon her, and the kids, and without
question the dog!

Understand, I did not stop believing in Jesus. But I did stop
believing that *I* could ever have *victory* in Jesus.

Now, it is a good exercise for me to analyze such an event.
The meltdown is over, and I am still here. The sun rose this morning,
and God is still in His Heaven. I can be a bit objective now, and try
to learn from it all.

Perhaps you are never prone to such an occurrence. But your
family member may be. In the cooler temperature of today, as I

consider the anatomy of my spiritual meltdown, I offer the following brief observations and advice.

1) I had just finished a week or two having experienced some tough spiritual battles which resulted in some real victories. I think Satan knows just when to attack us, and when we have just come off the pitch with a sense of victory and battle-fatigue, that is a sure time to be extra watchful.

2) I got mad at the dog (poor dog!). Then it spiraled into berating myself for having such a temper. It is then that the whispers come: "Where is the *joy* and *patience* you preach about?" "So much for *your* growth into Jesus-likeness," etc. God *convicts,* but Satan *condemns.* Such thoughts of hopelessness or uselessness are never from God.

3) When we blow it, we can feel grieved over our "loss" of righteousness. It is good then to remember that we never had any righteousness of our own to "lose" in the first place! We are indeed "*miserable* offenders" (as the Prayer Book says.) The far better thing to do rather than moan all day about our mess-up is to go to Jesus right away and let His blood cleanse us, enabling us to receive forgiveness and put on garments of praise. I realize that my berating of myself was not born in true repentance, but in a pride-based shame over my actions.

4) When a meltdown is looming, watch out for the "alwayses" and the "nevers" of despair, i.e. "I will *always* feel like this from now on; I have lost my victory forever." Or, "I will *never* get victory over my sin and self, just as well that I give up now." Don't listen to the "Alwayses" and the "Nevers." Their source is the pit of Hell itself.

5) Take great comfort in the truth that, for a Christian, *this life* is as *bad* as it gets. (For an unbeliever, *this life* is as *good* as it gets.) That is good to remember on a bad day. (It is also really good to remember on a good day!) Heaven and Jesus await every simple believer. What a comfort for a distraught soul!

6) The only true consolations for a Christian are to be found in Christ, His atoning Work and His sufficient Word. Even in the midst of a meltdown day, the Gospel is still the Gospel, and Christ will not abandon. If you can muster the strength, preach the Gospel to yourself in the midst of your meltdown. If you cannot, then when the first glimmers of hope begin to break through (perhaps through the ministry of a spouse or friend), receive them as a thirsty man does water. Restoration comes through repentance and cleansing by the blood of Christ, not by wallowing in one's failure.

> *Because of the Lord's great love we are not consumed,*
> *for his compassions never fail.*
> *They are new every morning;*
> *great is your faithfulness.*
> *I say to myself, "The Lord is my portion;*
> *therefore I will wait for him.*
> (Lamentations 3:22-24)

Well, I bless the Lord today for His mercies, which are indeed "new every morning."

Grace and Peace be Yours in Abundance Through our Lord and Saviour, Jesus Christ.

Be Encouraged!

Four Pillars in My Life

Then you will know the truth. Jesus answered, "I am the ... truth ... " John 8:32; 14:6

Dear Family In Christ,

In some ways, in the short-term, it is easier to be an atheist than a Christian. Atheists do not have to grapple with Ultimate Issues in the same way that believers do. If life is just a chance event in a meaningless universe, then issues such as suffering and tragedy simply do not carry the same weight for them. Theists, and especially Christians, have to grapple with seemingly unresolvable issues because they believe in a meaningful universe governed by a good God. As tough as that can be sometimes, the alternative - meaninglessness - is vastly worse in the long-term.

So, being a follower of Jesus has opened up *more* questions to me than I would have had otherwise. When the light is switched "on", you not only see more things, but you also become aware of so much that you cannot yet understand. My questions actually bring me a thrill, every bit as much as they may bring me consternation. I am thrilled by the mysteries of Christ and the Christian life, and I look forward with great anticipation to a day of deeper understanding - with a glorified mind - in Heaven.

As believers, we should never be afraid of questions born of a genuine mind and heart engaging with God and His Word. As Matthew Henry said, rather than despairing of our inability to plumb the depths of God and His ways (how could we?), we should sit on the brink and adore the depth of this Truth which we have begun to discover.

In the midst of all the mysteries of life as a believer, I offer the following four "pillars" upon which my life is built. Though simplistic, these four granite posts form a profoundly strong foundation for my life.

1) There is such a thing as Truth.

Don't overlook this. We live in an age that is telling us that there is no ultimate Truth. We are being told that all is relative, and nothing is therefore solid. To believe this is to believe that the Universe is a cold, lonely place. Anything goes if there is no Truth. Life can have no anchor, and in the end we are a race of blind, hopeless creatures in a cruel, meaningless cosmos.

Humans long for meaning and purpose. Just as the existence of a stomach presupposes the existence of food, so the existence of a mind to know and a heart to be satisfied presupposes the existence of Truth.

To assert that there is finally an absolute Truth is, in fact, a very powerful belief. It steadies the mind and the morals in a culture that is unraveling all about us.

2) Truth is Knowable.

It follows as a logical necessity, that if Truth exists, it must be *knowable,* or there is no point to it. Truth is not silent, but speaking. The universe is not mute. We can *know* the Truth, if not exhaustively, never-the-less, genuinely.

This means that we do not have to go through life in ignorance. This means that we can discover Meaning. This means that we can encounter Purpose.

Our culture today disdains such a notion. It is in fashion to be unsure. Ignorance can even become a convenient excuse for a sinful lifestyle. To suggest that Truth can be *known* is seen as arrogant or fool-hearty. But a Truth that is mute, hidden, bashful, is a worthless Truth, which might as well not even exist.

3) Jesus Christ is Truth.

Truth has manifested itself in Jesus of Nazareth. Truth not only exists, and is not only knowable, it is *Incarnate* in Jesus. And, it follows as a logical necessity that there must be a faithful account of

Jesus, or the entire Christ-event is of no use. So, I embrace the Bible (the Book which is about Jesus) as a true and faithful testimony to Jesus.

Again, our culture casts aspersions upon any suggestion that one can be *sure* in any absolute sense. But never confuse confidence with arrogance. Arrogance has to do with an oversized view of self. Confidence (the very root of the word is "fides" which is Latin for "faith"), in a Christian context assumes a looking away from oneself to Jesus Christ, and being sure of Him, not of ourselves. You will certainly fit into our current culture more easily if you are sure of nothing, but you will do society absolutely no good whatsoever.

4) The Bible is a Faithful Record of the Truth that is in Jesus Christ

It would be absurd - even cruel - for God to have acted in Truth in Jesus Christ, and then not left a faithful witness to that Truth. We would soon be in the dark again, trusting in hunches and fables. With just a little thought, you can see that the Bible is therefore *necessary*. Of course one can state the case for the Bible in many ways, and use stronger language than I have used here (words like God-breathed, without error), but all I am trying to do here is make plain that if the first three are true, the fourth is necessarily true.

When I read the Bible I encounter Jesus Christ, and, therefore, Truth. The Living Word becomes known through the written word, not through séances and folk tales!

There is much I don't know, much I will never know, but there are some things of which I am sure. So, dear friend in Jesus, I leave you with these pillars of my life, and I commend them to you that from the stability which they together offer, you may embrace the mysteries and endure the agonies of the questions which arise in the experience of every genuine follower of Jesus Christ.

Happy Following.

Be Encouraged!

Simple Obedience Produces Eternal Results

For He Himself is our peace.
Ephesians 2:14

Beloved,

How wonderful is the Kingdom of God! We marvel at the workings of God's grace. Jesus Christ is worthy of eternal and endless praise for His works without number in the hearts of men and women from every tribe, tongue, and nation.

I want to introduce you to a new hero of mine ... a trophy of God's grace with whom I have just become familiar. While I have not (yet) met him personally, I know something of his story, and I look forward with great anticipation to meeting Him one day in that Land of Endless Joy.

Meet Jacob Deshazer. While you may have never heard of him, just listen to his story.

Jacob was born in the USA in 1912. During the Second World War, he was a bombardier on a B25 airplane. In 1942, he, along with his aircrew of five and 23 other warplanes took off from the *USS Hornet* in a daring raid on Japan. While the mission was largely successful, he and the crew of his plane, *The Bat*, were forced to bail out over enemy territory and were all captured the next day.

Jacob Deshazer was to spend the next 40 months in a Japanese prison camp. Three of his crewmates were executed. Another was allowed to slowly starve to death.

Two years into his captivity, Jacob asked his captors to give him a Bible. He was not a Christian at the time. Receiving one, he began to read the Word of God, and before long, God opened his heart to see Jesus as His Saviour.

He read in Romans 10:9, "If you confess with you mouth 'Jesus is Lord', and believe in your heart that God raised Him from the dead, you shall be saved." So he did, and so he was!

Immediately Jacob began to treat his captors with respect. God had changed his heart and given him a new nature!

After the war, Jacob went to Bible College in Seattle, but only to *return to Japan* in 1948 as a missionary. He wrote a little pamphlet for the Japanese people entitled *I Was a Prisoner in Japan.* One day, still in 1948, a distinguished Japanese man named Mitsuo Fuchida was walking through the streets of Tokyo when someone placed one of these tracts in his hands. Mitsuo was distinguished in Japanese society, for it was *he* who had led the aerial attack on Pearl Harbor in 1941. The testimony of Jacob Deshazer pierced his heart! However, Bibles were scarce in post-war Japan, and Mitsuo would have to wait until the Spring of 1949, whilst walking past the very same spot in Tokyo, for a missionary from the Pocket Testament League to offer him a Bible.

Mitsuo Fuchida eagerly gobbled up the Word of Life and was converted to Christ.

The next year, in 1950, he met Jacob Deshazer, who by then was holding evangelistic meetings throughout Japan, preaching the Good News of Jesus to crowds numbering into the tens of thousands. They became immediate friends. What marvelous things grace can do!

The two preached together.

Mitsuo toured the USA speaking of the love and mercy of God through Jesus Christ, even as Jacob toured Japan.

In 1959, Jacob Deshazar moved with his wife and children to Nagoya, Japan, the very city he had bombed. There he planted a church which he served for 30 years. The next year Mitsuo became a citizen of the USA, the very country he had bombed, living amongst and preaching to those who had formerly been his enemies. He even wrote a book entitled *From Pearl Harbor to Calvary.*

I write this little true story to encourage us all in the wonderful power of the Gospel of Jesus Christ, especially when accompanied by simple obedience. It is impossible to measure the results which simple obedience will bring. I fear that we sometimes believe that only profound heroic measures will produce results that count in God's eyes. Ponder the chain of simple, obedient events that led to the conversions of these two men:

*How did that first Bible even find its way into the prison camp in 1944?

*Who left it there? Perhaps another POW, a believer, since deceased, had it amidst his gear.

*Who was that faithful Christian worker, known only perhaps to the Lord, and famous only before His Throne, who handed out Jacob's testimonial tract to an unsuspecting, but spiritually hungry Mitsuo Fuchida in 1948?

*Did he ever know of the "God-incidence" that happened when he handed the booklet to "just another" passer-by?

*What about that faithful soul from the Pocket Testament League who was available for God to use in the Spring of 1949?

*I wonder how he felt going to witness and work that day. Did he have any sense of the significance of his labours on that one fateful spring morning? We never know what eternal impact we might have in seemingly insignificant acts of faithfulness!

I am not ashamed of the Gospel, because it is the power of God for the salvation of everyone who believes: first for the Jew, then for the Gentile. (Romans 1:16)

May we all be encouraged today in the Glorious Gospel of Jesus Christ!

Be Encouraged!

God Really Loves Sinners

Jacob I loved, but Esau I hated.
Romans 9:13

Brothers and Sisters, Loved in Christ,

If you dwell upon the above passage, reading it in the context of the entirety of Romans, chapter 9, and then chapter 9 in the entirety of the Book of Romans, and then Romans in the entirety of the Bible itself, you realize what a truly shocking passage it is.

Step back with me and survey the seven words "Jacob I loved, but Esau I hated" in their setting.

First, within their setting of the whole Bible: The Bible is a book about God's Son, Jesus, and His amazing, awesome, free workings to redeem all of fallen creation solely by His grace, and finally for His glory. Not one human deserved redemption, but the Bible's Big Story tells us that God has moved in sovereign grace to save through His Son.

Next, in the context of the Book of Romans: Romans tells us the unimaginably profound news that God's redemption of our rebel race has been accomplished through the substitution of His Son, Jesus. He actually bore the wrath we deserved. No one merits this, and God did not have to do it. He did it for His enemies, while they were yet His enemies.

Finally, in the setting of Romans, Chapter 9: We learn that God's love never has been, and never will be compelled by anything outside of God Himself. In other words, *we* cannot "make" God love us. He will never owe us love. His love is sovereign, free, unhindered by our sinfulness, and undeserved. Its source and spring is in His very own inscrutable, wise counsel and will. In Romans 9, it is *God* who has the free will (bet you never thought of it that way!).

Now look at the above seven words with me again: "Jacob I loved, but Esau I hated." What we tend to think is that there must have been something lovable about Jacob, something inherently cute, some righteousness which irresistibly drew God towards him, and compelled God to love him.

We don't like to think at all about God hating Esau, but if we must, we make it more palatable by imagining that Esau must have been, by comparison to Jacob (and, of course, to us!), a particularly dastardly character. There *must*, we think, have been something compelling in Jacob and repelling in Esau. If this was a Hollywood "western" Jacob would be in a white hat, Esau in a black.

But ... in so thinking, we have just fallen into the trap of man-centred, rather than God-centred religion, which is somehow built upon *us*, *our* performance, *our* righteousness, *we* being by comparison better than others.

What is truly shocking in the above passage is that God ... *loved Jacob*! Go back and read the narrative in Genesis, beginning in chapter 25. Jacob was a complete creep! He was a deceiver and a manipulator. He comes off no better than Esau, who was himself no choir boy. They both deserved black hats!

I would not find it at all shocking if I read that God, a Holy, righteous, sin- hating God, could not stand *both* Jacob and Esau (and me too, frankly). But the Bible tells us the stunning news that God loved Jacob:

"STOP PRESS: GOD LOVED JACOB!"

And what Romans 9 wants to get into our heads is that God's incredible, undeserved love is not compelled by our works, but by God's mercy alone: "It does not, therefore, depend upon man's desire or effort, but on God's mercy." (Romans 9:16)

I feel much better having salvation dependent upon an all wise God who cannot be bought off, rather than upon wicked, sinful men who cannot trust even themselves.

Now, we have to deal with the question which most of you are probably puzzling over: "How can God hate *anybody*, let alone Esau?" We can try to tone it down with platitudes like "God loves the sinner but hates the sin," but the seven words are there, and we cannot shake them off. The fact is, no one, not Esau, you, or I *deserves* the love of God. We deserve the wrath of God. Period. God is not in debt to any human, so that He *must* love them in a saving way.

What the Seven words "Jacob I loved, but Esau I hated" mean is that God loved Jacob - rather than Esau - in a covenantal, saving sense. And, because He set His saving covenant upon Jacob, He was actually a lot tougher in this life upon Jacob than upon his big brother Esau. He gave Esau an immediate inheritance, the entire region of Seir, and his people became very powerful in an earthly sense. But He took Jacob down to Egypt as a slave, and His people became powerless, with God as their only treasure and hope. (Joshua 24:4) That's called "love" in the redemptive, biblical sense.

So: here is the BIG DEAL: God loves because He is amazing, not because we are. I know this might spoil your party, but it will also set you free. The most famous Bible verse of all, John 3:16, tells us that "... God so loved the world, that He sent His one and only Son ...." The amazing thing about this verse, taken in the context of the whole Bible, is not that God loves the world because the world is lovable, but that God loves an unlovable world, a world which hates Him, and would kill Him if given half the chance. I am not loved by God because *I* have performed well, but because of God's free, sovereign grace. It is *Christ* who has performed well, in dying for my sins on a cruel cross. This is a profoundly freeing Truth.

Finally, you know the first verse of the most famous hymn ever:

Amazing Grace! How sweet the sound that saved a wretch like me!

Be careful that you are not offended by the truth of that word *wretch*. Do not rewrite that hymn to sentimentally say:

Amazing Me! How sweet I am. No wonder God Loves Me!

146

God's love is profound, free, amazing, unhindered, uncompelled, unstoppable, irresistible, unshakable, unbreakable, eternal, tough, made to last, and undeserved.

Yours … Amazingly.

Be Encouraged!

God is Warning our Wicked, Forgetful World

As it was in the days of Noah, so will it be at the coming of the Son of Man. For in the days before the flood, people were eating and drinking, marrying and giving in marriage, up to the day Noah entered the ark, and they knew nothing about what would happen until the flood came and took them all away.
Matthew 24:37-39

Dear Family in Christ,

Many, many years ago I read a sermon by Bishop J. C. Ryle called "What Worldliness Forgets." It was based upon the above text, and I found it challenging and instructive. I actually rewrote it when I was a very young preacher and preached it many times (don't worry, I gave credit to the great bishop!).

While that original sermon was timely for the mid-nineteenth century, how much more timely is that old sermon for the generation in which we live!

How did the Lord Jesus describe Noah's generation? The great trademark of Noah's society, according to the Lord Jesus in the passage above, could be summed up in one word: "forgetful." Look with me at the description of the people of Noah's day.

They were:

Eating

Drinking

Marrying

Now, at face value, there was nothing *wrong* with what they were doing. There is certainly nothing wrong with eating, drinking, and marrying. The problem was that was *all* they were doing.

Their lives had become thoroughly secular ... Being merely lived on the "horizontal" plane.

While consumed with eating, drinking, marrying, giving in marriage, they had forgotten some very important things:

That they had souls.

That there was an Eternity.

That there was a God.

Life, for those who were living up until the very day in which Noah entered the ark, had become:

Easy, Carefree,

Cozy, Thoughtless

Who needed God? Who needed to pray? Why spoil the party with thoughts of Eternity, accountability, judgment? The stock market was up, the kids were at Uni. All was well.

Now, it is vital that we get *God's mind* on that society:

The Lord saw how great man's wickedness on the earth had become, and that every inclination of the thoughts of his heart was only evil all the time. (Genesis 6:5)

God saw such a secular society as *wicked*. A culture which had no room for its Creator, a people who forgot that they had *souls*, a generation committed only to the *now*, God deemed as *evil* "all the time."

Noah's peers ripened themselves for judgment by their forgetfulness ... their deliberate forgetfulness ... of who they really were: Human beings, living souls, image bearers of God Himself.

They thought themselves fine without God. Invincible. Modern. Come of Age. But they were in line for a great outpouring of Wrath, and oblivious to it. Right up to and until the day that Noah entered the ark, and "the flood came and took them all away."

Now, the description of society in the Days of Noah, Jesus says, will be an apt description of society just at the return of Jesus Christ, the Last Judgment, the end of the Age, and the inauguration of the Kingdom of God. It will not necessarily be that we will all be outwardly "bad," just forgetful ... deliberately forgetful.

Cool. Modern.

European. Secular.

Prayerless.

God calls such a soulless culture:

Wicked.(Genesis 6:5)

And He intends to judge such a culture.

Brothers and sisters, from Jesus' own words we can deduce that the "coming of the Son of Man" is indeed nigh. How urgent it is that *we* be not forgetful of the Lord, our souls, Eternity, the Brevity of Time, and of the reality of a swift and thorough judgment upon our wicked race!

A culture which cannot think past the weekend is, in God's mind, a wicked culture. A generation which erases the soul is an evil generation.

Be not fooled by the "coolness" of the Age in which we live. It is ripe for Judgment. Pursue Christ with all your heart. Remember that you have a soul for which Jesus died, which will live on the day your body dies and give an account to the God who made it.

Leave off sin and run after holiness. Warn your friends - with tears. Pray for our generation. Be about Kingdom living. Live in Time, but with an eye ever on Eternity.

Yours for Jesus, Who is "at the Door."

Be Encouraged!

Our Sin-Hating God is Making You A Sin-Hater Like Him

Let those who love the Lord hate evil.
Psalm 97:10

Dear Friend,

The Bible cannot put it more plainly. God is not "beating about the bush."

Let those who love the Lord hate evil.

Loving the Lord implies and requires that we abhor evil - every manifestation of it in our hearts, words, attitudes, actions, homes, families, and society. The God of the Bible, the God Who Is There, is a Beautiful, Pure, Unimpeachable, Sin-Hating God. He always has been, and He always will be.

He cannot lie ... ever, in any way. His eyes are too pure to look upon evil. He cannot be tempted to do wrong. He will never change.

In terms of His Absolute Goodness, He is as different from us human beings as it is possible to be. He is at the other end of the spectrum. He is not even *on* the spectrum.

Now, whenever Jesus begins to work in a sinful soul, one of the sure signs that Grace is present is an awareness and increasing hatred of sin. Indeed, Jesus said that one of the key things that His Holy Spirit would do, would be to "convict ... of sin." (John 16:8)

The awakened soul becomes a soul that:

Is aware of sin ... like it never used to be ... Sin within and without.

The awakened soul becomes a soul that:

Is beginning to hate sin ... especially its own ...

An awakened soul becomes a soul that:

Loves goodness and righteousness ... even if it cannot live up to what it loves.

An awakened soul becomes a soul that:

Is alive to God ... and therefore dead to sin (or at least yearns to be).

Beloved, we are saved *to*, as well as *from*. Yes, we are wonderfully saved *from* sin, its penalty, pollution, and power. Ah, but we are also saved *to* God, His Holiness, Loveliness, and Purity.

Therefore, let us not deceive ourselves. Each must examine his own heart in this most important matter. If you love the Lord, you must turn from evil. You must become a true repenter. You must ask God to give you a heart for holiness. The Lord promises a New Heart. Ask Him for one! Plead for a sensitive conscience. Get on your knees and ask God to help you hate sin. Don't try to see "how much sin you can get away with" and still follow Jesus. Long to be like Jesus. Ask God to search your heart. Ask God to give you a new love for Truth and Goodness and Purity. Ask God to do a Psalm 2:11 move on you:

Serve the Lord with fear and rejoice with trembling.

God will surely do a deep and beautiful work of Grace in each and every one who earnestly seeks true Holiness of Heart and Life. There may be real battles with sin, but a victory will be sure.

Augustine said it well:

Lord Command what You will, but then Give what You Command.

Don't Settle For Less! In the end, each of us is as holy (and therefore happy!) as we want to be.

Create in Me a Clean Heart, O God, and renew a right spirit in me.
(Psalm 51:10 KJV)

Yours For Holiness of Heart and Life.

Be Encouraged!

God Will Reduce You For His Glory and Your Good

The sun rose above him as he passed Peniel, and he was limping because of his hip.
Genesis 32:31

Beloved in Grace,

Let me ask you a few questions:

*How badly do you want to be changed?

*How desperate are you for holiness of heart and life?

*Which would be worse for you: 1) To have cancer or, 2) To never desire to read your Bible and draw near to Jesus?

*If the Lord, in His sovereign love and grace, were to afflict you, but in so doing, *transform* you, would you consider such an affliction to be worth it?

*Would you rather get to a place where you treasure Jesus supremely, even if it cost you something very dear, or hold onto the dear thing, at the cost of sweetness with Christ?

Meet Jacob: Chosen of God ... a very dangerous thing! Jacob is deceitful, cunning, cowardly, and forever on the run. He is a man of sweat and natural strength. You would not want him as your friend. His very name means "heel grabber" or, by implication, "deceiver."

But, Jacob is, nevertheless, chosen of God. God's covenant and promise – for reasons known only to God - rest upon Jacob ...

154

sovereignly … in spite of his unworthiness … apparently for nothing "good" in Jacob.

God is not going to let Jacob alone. God is going to change him. God is going to win him.

In Genesis, chapter 32, Jacob, the "heel grabber," the "deceiver," wrestles with God. The one who is always on the run is now tackled and brought to the dust from whence he came. God won't be beaten. In subduing the rebel, God puts Jacob's hip out of place. (Imagine the *pain!*)

As the sun rises, Jacob, now renamed Israel, which means "wrestles with God," limps away … never to be the same.

He is crippled, but whole.
No longer does he run. He can't.
There is no more deception, pride, lying.

The Jacob/Israel we see for the rest of the story is a person you would want to befriend. There is now a *godliness* about the man with the limp. You can see the change in him when you read the story. He has been subdued by God; reduced by the Almighty. He does not lie any more. He is no longer crafty. He can sleep at night. There is now something about him that coheres with being Chosen of God. No longer striding and strutting, but limping and loving, there's something genuine about Jacob/Israel that is consistent with a person who is encountering God.

If we will do well in this life with Jesus, in this state of "chosen-ness," then we must get it straight once and for all that God is concerned for our holiness *before* our happiness. Happiness, the deep kind, the kind that only Jesus ever gives, comes later. He who has set His love upon us will have our *hearts*. Not until our hearts are His can we experience anything like the happiness for which we have been chosen.

And, like Jacob, we are people of sweat, and strength, and craft, and intrigue, always on the move, always scheming and machining our way through life. And, as in Jacob's case, God won't have it. He loves us too much. He loves His own Glory too much. (He is the only One in the Universe who can rightly and safely do this.) He will wound us with His love if He must and not apologize for it. He never said "sorry" to Jacob.

It is all on His terms.
Never on ours.

He knows what is best for us, though we are often too foolish to appreciate such. He wills our sanctification, which can only happen when we are supremely satisfied in Jesus. And, if becoming supremely satisfied in Jesus means that God must wound us, if that is what it will take to make us stop running and maneuvering, so be it. God knows the price is well worth it.

So, I ask you again: How serious are you about this Salvation thing? You need to deal with that question, because God is very serious about it ...

Just ask Jacob. He's easy to find ... He's the guy with the limp.

Yours limping For Jesus.

Be Encouraged!

Jesus Really Is Worth Everything

The kingdom of heaven is like treasure hidden in a field.
When a man found it, he hid it again, and then in his joy went and
sold all he had and bought that field.
Matthew 13:44

A Little Boy had a dream. It was a wonderful dream. It was the best dream he had ever had.

In his dream the Little Boy was in the middle of the most wonderful toyshop in all the world.

With ever widening eyes he scanned the shelves and aisles, finding it impossible to absorb.

In his dream the Wonderful Man Who Owned the Shop appeared.

"Little boy," he said, "I am so glad you are here in my wonderful shop. I want to tell you what I plan to do for you, Little Boy."

The Little Boy's eyes grew even wider, his heart began to pound, his mouth got dry. "See all these toys?" said the Wonderful Man Who Owned the Shop. " Well, you can have them *all*. They are *all* for you!"

The Little Boy could not believe what he was hearing.

"Or," said the Wonderful Man Who Owned the Shop, "you can have this *one* toy." From behind his back, as if by magic, the Wonderful Man Who Owned the Shop brought out a smallish box, wrapped like a gift.

"This," said the Wonderful Man Who Owned the Shop to the Little Boy, " is the most wonderful toy of all. *This* toy will give you more joy than all these other toys put together. You will *never* get tired of *this* toy."

The Little Boy could hardly contain his excitement. He wanted *all* the toys in the shop, *and* the most wonderful toy of all! The Little Boy's dream just kept getting better and better.

"Now," said the Wonderful Man Who Owned the Shop, "you have to make a choice."

The Little Boy was so full of excitement that he could not even speak. In his dream he kept trying to talk, but no words would come out.

"You can have *all* the toys in my shop," said the Wonderful Man Who Owned the Shop, "*or*, you can have the most wonderful toy of all. But you cannot have both. The choice is yours."

The Little Boy looked at the shelves bursting with toys. He looked at the box in the Wonderful Man Who Owned the Shop's hands. Questions raced through the Little Boy's mind. He wondered if it could really be true that *one* toy could be better than *all* the other toys put together. How could the Wonderful Man Who Owned the Shop *know* for sure what would make the Little Boy happy? He even wondered if he could trust the Wonderful man Who Owned the Shop to tell him the truth ... Maybe he was not a wonderful man, but a bad, stingy man who didn't really want the Little Boy to have fun ...

"The choice is yours," said the Wonderful Man Who Owned the Shop.

The Little Boy looked again at all the toys. He looked again at the smallish box. His hands were sweaty.

"It is time to choose," said the Wonderful Man Who Owned the Shop, a big smile on his face.

The Little Boy opened his mouth to speak ...Just then the Little Boy's mother turned on his light and opened the curtains ...

There is a great paradox in the Christian Life:

Jesus Christ offers Himself *freely*:

Come unto Me all you who are weary and burdened.
(Matthew 11:28)

But He costs *everything:*

If anyone would come after Me, he must deny himself, take up his cross daily, and follow Me. (Luke 9:23)

You can have Jesus, as your all sufficient Treasure, freely given, but it will cost you everything else, even your very self.

OR

You can have your life, and all the world thrown in, but it will cost you Jesus.

You cannot have both. That is just the way it is. It is no dream; it is Reality.That is the paradox of the Way to Heaven ... Free, but at the highest cost ...

Again:

If anyone would come after me, he must deny himself and take up his cross and follow me. For whoever wants to save his life will lose it, but whoever loses his life for me will save it. (Luke 9:23-24)

Weigh it up, count the cost, make the choice ... Every day.

Yours, For the Treasure that is Jesus Christ.

Be Encouraged!

Our Jesus is a Sadness-Bearing Saviour

Surely he hath borne our griefs, and carried our sorrows.
Isaiah 53:4 KJV

Beloved in Christ,

It is impossible to live this life and be free from pain and sorrow. Without question, the deepest and most bitter pain is the pain caused by relationships. The pain which our bodies know is not to be compared with the sorrow that our hearts know.

What do we do with sorrow? Where do we put it? How can we deal with it?

There are three things that you can do with your sorrow. Two of them are destructive; one of them is redemptive.

Let's look at these three in turn.

1) You can *stuff it.*

Many do this. Many take their pain and sorrow and stuff it way down inside. Down in their hearts their pain begins to putrefy and turn gangrenous. It slowly poisons the soul. It is sure to produce malice, bitterness of spirit, and sadness of soul. Pain-stuffed hearts produce sad, depressed, despondent people.

2) You can *vent it.*

Again, many do this. Many take their pain and turn it into aggression towards others. Their anger seems to always be simmering just beneath the surface. People do what they do because of pain. Aggressive, short-fused people are often hurting people. Words become venomous and relationships seem to always be in jeopardy.

The old adage is true: Hurt People ... hurt people.

Well, neither of the above two options are good choices. But there is another option ... a good one that actually can turn sorrow into a redemptive event in one's life:

3) You can *give it*.

There is actually One upon whom you can roll your sorrow, pain, and sadness. The Lord Jesus is not only a sin-bearing Saviour, He is a sadness - bearing friend. That is exactly what Isaiah 53:4 tells us. We all rejoice (I hope) in the wonderful truth that Jesus Christ bore our sins upon His body on the cross. But our verse at the top of this letter tells us that Jesus has also carried our sadness. This truth can and should be life- transforming.

When you give Jesus your pain and sorrow, they become *Redemptive.* The Lord Jesus Himself uses your pain and sorrow, given to Him, to bring you to a new place of trust, rest, joy and peace in Him.

Our Jesus is the One who invites saying:

Come unto Me all who are weary and burdened and I will give you rest. (Matthew 11:28)

He is the One called our "Sympathetic High Priest."He is called the "Man of sorrows, acquainted with grief." He is the One upon whom you are urged to "Cast all your cares, for He cares for you."

Don't stuff it ...

Don't vent it ...

As often as it hurts ... GIVE IT

The Spirit of the Lord God is upon me; because the Lord hath anointed me to preach good tidings unto the meek; he hath sent me to bind up the brokenhearted, to proclaim liberty to the captives, and the opening of the prison to them that are bound;

To proclaim the acceptable year of the Lord, and the day of vengeance of our God; to comfort all that mourn;

To appoint unto them that mourn in Zion, to give unto them beauty for ashes, the oil of joy for mourning, the garment of praise for the spirit of heaviness; that they might be called trees of righteousness, the planting of the Lord, that he might be glorified. (Isaiah 61:1-3 KJV)

What a Saviour is our Jesus!

Yours, Forever Grateful for Jesus.

Be Encouraged!

God Won't Let You Get Away With Grumbling

You grumbled in your tents ...
Deuteronomy 1:27

Dear Church,

In a sense, the parting of the Red Sea that Israel might be delivered from bondage in Egypt was the easy part of becoming God's Redeemed People.

Learning to live in loving, thankful relationship with Yahweh and one another was much harder.

The journey from Egypt to the Promised land of Canaan should have taken two weeks.

It took forty years.

It was not the rough terrain that delayed Israel's arrival. Nor was it the numerous hostile tribes along the way.

God delayed them.

He delayed them because of their hard, faithless, fault-finding, ungrateful hearts. He gave them forty years of futile wandering ...'round and around in circles ...in the desert ... until all the grumblers were dead.

The verse above, recounted by Moses near the end of his life just as leadership was to be passed to Joshua at the end of the forty years of futility, sums up the sinful hearts of the people of Israel, the very ones whom God had Redeemed from slavery:

You grumbled in your tents ...

163

What a pathetic picture! God's Redeemed People, brought out of slavery by the hand of God! The very People who should have been thankful, grateful, and always praising, had become a group of moaners and groaners. Again:

You grumbled in your tents ...

Notice with me what God noticed (I think this is really significant): It was "in their tents" that they grumbled. That is, they had become moaners at home about God and the way he was doing things. When they got home from church, they complained about it. Instead of their tents being filled with praise and thankfulness, they were places of fault-finding and nit-picking. There was just a general spirit amongst the people of thanklessness. Those who should have been the most joyous people on earth (Saved! Delivered! Free! Promise-Land bound!) were sitting around after dinner in their tents complaining about the way things were. You can imagine them lying about on their pillows, just moaning. Just a short time before, they had been in the cruelty of Egyptian bondage.

The kids heard their parents complaining ...

Even more, *God* heard the people complaining. He was the Unseen Listener in every household!

The Book of Numbers details their complaining. It makes for instructive (how *not* to be), but not pleasant, reading. In the ungrateful minds of the people, nothing was good enough. Moses could do nothing to their standard ... and, by implication, neither could Moses' boss ... God.

Now, God *judged* these people for being grumblers. It was an offense to Him. These were the people of God, but they were acting like spoiled children. God *heard* it and *judged* it. He doomed them to futility. No reaching their potential for them. They all perished in the wilderness ... complaining all the while.

The Book of Romans tells us that "these things" have been "written to teach us" (15:4). If there is one group of people who should be even more grateful to God for deliverance than those ancient Israelites, it is we who name the Name of Jesus Christ.

* Like them, we have been delivered from bondage, not to the Egyptians, but to sin.

* Like them, we have been set free from tyranny, not just from slave owners with whips, but from Satan himself.

* Like them, we have a destiny, but not merely a patch of land on earth, but Glory itself.

We should be the most thankful people on earth.

But are we? Are we not also prone towards "grumbling in our tents"? Do we not find it all too easy, perhaps even perversely enjoyable, to complain about:

> Our spouses
> (not sexy enough, don't understand, no fun, etc.)
> Our kids
> (too slow, too fast, too lazy, too demanding, etc.)
> Our churches
> (music, sermons, members, etc.)

God hears.

God will judge.

The New Testament exhorts the People of God to:

Do everything without complaining. (Philippians 2:14)
Give thanks in all circumstances. (1 Thessalonians 5:18)
Be joyful always. (1 Thessalonians 5:16)

It is wicked to grumble. It takes no faith to be a complainer. Moaning requires no spiritual effort.

The miracle of our Redemption should so impact our thinking, feeling, dreaming, and living that grumbling and complaining simply can have no place any longer in our lives.

May the Lord Jesus forgive us for any ungratefulness of heart, attitude, and speech. May we be a truly happy and grateful People, voicing our gratitude, and living every day with the tyranny of sin behind us, and the anticipation of Glory before us.

There is simply no other way for Redeemed People.

Thankfully Yours.

Be Encouraged!

Only Jesus Preserves Nations From Tyranny

So if the Son sets you free, you shall be free indeed.
John 8:36

Beloved In Christ,

I want to reflect with you for just a moment upon a trip which Tessa and I made recently to an Eastern European country.

It was a great joy to share with and preach the wonders of Jesus to fellow brothers and sisters, servants of Jesus Christ, in that formerly communist land. How precious is the unity which we have as believers, right across borders and cultures!

The men and women with whom we shared fellowship had lived decades under Soviet communism. They retold stories of the regular visits from the communist officials to the church gatherings, just to keep track of what was happening. They told of having to report the names and the movements of members to the State.

Food was often scarce.They had little freedom to relocate, change jobs, travel (even within the Soviet Bloc). Housing was assigned by the State.Shops were half-filled, and all goods were utilitarian ... no luxuries, little beauty.

Then, in the late 1980's came the winds of change. In came political revolution and the overthrow of the Soviet system. It seemed to be a dream! Freedom to determine one's future, to grow and develop as individuals, to gain wealth, to dream and stretch was suddenly the possession of millions of people across Eastern Europe.

Today, the streets of Warsaw and Gdansk, Budapest and Moscow look like the streets in any Western city. Shops are full, people are bustling to and from their appointments, and a sense of wealth pervades the air.

There is so much that is good. Without a doubt freedom has brought many blessings. But, I sat at table with a man about my age, an elder in a church, a man with a decent job and a reasonable future. He was a follower of Jesus. He said without equivocation that life, not at a surface level, but at a deep level, was better under the communists. I asked him just what he meant.

He said that people have not handled their freedom well. Families under communism were close, because life was tough. Churches were strong because believing in Jesus was costly. Communities functioned in a spirit of interdependence, because in times of scarcity, there was no other way to survive.

There was a preciousness to life that the Communist State could not overthrow.

But secular, materialistic, godless freedom is threatening to do what communism could not do:

Destroy families...

Ruin communities ...

Empty churches ...

We spoke together about the fact that democracy, this strange and rare experiment in self-government, simply cannot work if the populace as a whole does not have an inner moral gyroscope; if individuals do not have an inner sense of right and wrong, and a willingness to do what is right. We agreed that freedom has nothing to do with being free to do anything you wish, but that it has all to do with being free to live responsibly, to make wise choices.

Freedom requires responsibility, or it turns into selfishness and leads to the ruin of society. My dinner companion feared that he saw such social ruin on the horizon.

In the end, true freedom thrives in societies where Jesus Christ is honored in individual hearts and corporately revered in a nation's mindset. Neither atheism nor secularism are seedbeds in which freedom can flourish. Without God in the hearts and thoughts of the men and women, boys and girls who make up a society, freedom quickly turns into anarchy.

England, America, and few other countries have been able to live with remarkable freedom for these brief centuries because the Gospel has deeply penetrated society. God has deemed it safe to allow our societies the rare treasure of self-government. But as we deliberately and continually move away from the God who makes freedom possible and safe, the degradation of culture will be inevitable.

There are two options for our future, and only two: One: We will have the spiritual awakening that we desperately need, restoring Christ in the hearts of millions, and bringing a general sense of "God" throughout the culture. Two: We will experience what godless cultures inevitably and necessarily experience ... the loss of liberty, and the increase of totalitarian rule by those who are bigger than we are.

We will either experience a moral/spiritual revolution, or the day will come when our doors may be kicked in by the State. Either one will result in the strengthening of the Church, the treasuring of the family, and the valuing of communities. Either one is better than the social anarchy toward which our careless abuse of freedom is dragging us.

God is sovereign, and He will do what is best – for His glory and our good. Pray, and tell people about Jesus. There is no other hope for a free society.

Yours, Praying.

Be Encouraged!

The Lord is Changing you from a "When" to a "Wait" Person

On one occasion, while he was eating with them, he gave them this command: "Do not leave Jerusalem, but wait for the gift my Father promised, which you have heard me speak about. For John baptised with water, but in a few days you will be baptised with the Holy Spirit." ... Then they gathered round him and asked him, "Lord, are you at this time going to restore the kingdom to Israel?"

Acts 1:4-6

People of Grace,

Just before Jesus ascended into Heaven, He commanded His disciples to "wait" for the promised Holy Spirit. (Acts 1:4,5)

The disciples responded to a "Wait" command with a "When" question (v.6). In this context, "wait" and "when" are exact opposites. Let me explain. "Wait," received as a command from Jesus and obeyed, means:

"Lord, I want to hear and receive and do Your Agenda for me. I want to be in a place of trust and reliance upon You. I am weak and in need of your power. This is what I seek."

"Wait" is a Kingdom word, and speaks of a Kingdom way. "When," insisted on in preference to the Lord's "wait" means: "I have an agenda, Lord, and I want you to meet it. I need to get on with things, and You, Lord, are delaying me. I've programs and ideas, and I'm confident that I can achieve them."

"When" is a worldly word and speaks of a worldly way.

"Wait" is a humbling word.

170

"When" is a self-assured word.

"Wait" says "Lord I want to be effective."

"When" says "Lord I want to get busy."

"Wait" moves at the command of God.

"When" rushes as it pursues its own agenda.

"Wait" leaves a trail of blessing for others.

"When" leaves a wake of bruised and broken relationships.

As Eugene Peterson says, the disciples' "when" question "sounds suspiciously like "when will we get our kingdom assignments so that we can start running things?"

Now, "waiting" is not passive. Not where Jesus and His Kingdom are concerned. "Waiting for the Lord" is not like waiting for a bus ... It is active. It involves seeking Him in His Word. It means divesting ourselves of ... ourselves. It is listening. It is real soul work. The Bible is full of the stories of godly "waiters": Simeon "waiting" for the "consolation of Israel" (Luke 2:25), the Psalmist who, when in dire straits, "waited patiently for the Lord" (Psalm 40:1). Such "waiters' were not lie-abouts, but in fact God-attentive people of faith who became our spiritual giants.

"Waiting" acknowledges the sovereign Lordship of Jesus, and our utter dependence upon Him. We are positioned where He can bless us with no danger that we will think we were the cause of success, or the source of power. It keeps us out of the way, and safeguards us from ourselves.

You can tell a "when" person, or church, by their busyness and programmes.

You can tell a "wait" person, or church, by their effectiveness.

The rest of the Book of Acts chronicles for us that these first disciples, who learned to "wait," became world-changers. They did works of power. Prayer became their common language.

Satan would be happy for us to be "when" people. Self-reliant, insisting upon our agenda, imploring God to serve our ideas, busy, and burned out.

Jesus wants to be our Sovereign, good Lord, leading us to do His works in His ways. He invites us to be God-attentive, prayerful "waiters." In so becoming, we will actually find that prayer saves time, as Jesus Himself empowers us and leads us to do the things He has ordained for us to do.

May the Lord Jesus give, and may we receive, Grace to "wait."

Yours ... waiting.

Be Encouraged!

Our Jesus is Better Than All Others

How is your Beloved better than others ...?
Song of Solomon 5:9

Friend in Christ,

"How is your beloved better than others?"

So asked the "friends" to the "bride" in the love song we know as the Song of Solomon. We now see this ancient love sonnet between a bridegroom and his bride as an echo of the Greater Love Song between the Lord Jesus and His Church. And so, the question asked of a simple bride concerning her groom becomes for us a vital question about our attitude concerning the Lord Jesus Himself:

"How is your Jesus better than all the others?"

Now, in our Old Testament love sonnet, our bride does not have to dither about for an answer. She does not fumble her words. There is no shrug of the shoulders combined with a mumbled "I dunno ..." She launches into a six verse exalted description of "her man" with an "I was hoping you would ask" zeal. Her praiseful description begins with the soaring, " My beloved is *dazzling*, he is *outstanding among ten-thousand*" (v5:10), and ends with the cherishing words, "This is my beloved, this is my friend"(5:16).

No wonder that, by the end of her joyous description, the once skeptical, questioning friends now ask: "Where is he?" (6:1) meaning, "We want to meet this most wonderful of men!"

Application for us is obvious. The world about us is asking: "What is so special about Jesus? How is He any better than ...(fill in the blank) ... Mohammed, Buddha, etc?" Our friends see us following Jesus, some of us making radical decisions because of Him, and they have a right to wonder and ask: "What is the big deal about Jesus?"

173

Now, we need to have an answer to our friends' question. Our bride in the love sonnet had a ready response. She could articulate her heart to her friends. She *knew* her man. She waxed poetic. Many of our hymn-writers have done the same. But as I have no competence in poetry, allow me to wax doctrinal. I want to offer you seven Truths about Jesus Christ that set Him apart from all the others who would vie for the affection of our hearts and the allegiance of our lives. The following seven (and there could be untold others) answer the question, "How is your Jesus better than all others?" conclusively.

1) Jesus Christ is Himself God Eternal, co-eternal with the Father and the Holy Spirit.

The Son is the radiance of God's glory, and the exact representation of His being. (Hebrews 1:3)

2) Jesus Christ in Himself is Life. He possesses Life and lends it to all His Creation.

In Him was Life. (John 1:4)

He is before all things and in Him all things hold together. (Colossians 1:17)

3) Jesus Christ, the Eternal Son of the Eternal Father, is the Creator of everything that is.

Through Him all things were made; without Him nothing was made that has been made. (John 1:3)

4) Jesus Christ is the Redeemer. Incarnated. Crucified. Buried. Risen. Exalted.

For Christ died for sins, once for all, the righteous for the unrighteous, to bring you to God. (1 Peter 3:18)

5) Jesus Christ, together with the Father and the Spirit, is the sole possessor of all Wisdom, Truth, and Beauty.

... in whom are hidden all the treasures of wisdom and knowledge.
(Colossians 2:3)

6) Jesus Christ, together with the Father and the Spirit, is alone worthy of all our worship and adoration, now and forever.

To Him be glory both now and for ever. Amen! (2 Peter 3:18)

7) Jesus Christ, the carpenter from Nazareth, does and will rule the entire universe and beyond, everything seen and unseen, now and forever and ever.

To Him who sits on the throne, and to the Lamb, be praise and honour and glory and power forever and ever! (Revelation 5:13)

Well, each of the above is worthy of much meditation. Each, when pondered, will produce worship. Each sets Jesus Christ apart as "better than all others." You, with a bit of digging into your Bible, can come up with countless (literally, countless!) other attributes of Jesus Christ, our Beloved, which no other man, nor woman, however great, has ever, or ever will possess.

Indeed, our Saviour is "Dazzling" and "Outstanding among ten thousand."

"This is our Beloved."

"This is our friend."

When we are duly captivated by Him, the world will see, and in seeing, they will want to know more.

I encourage you to make it your life's goal to know and enjoy and adore and love and follow and trust and serve and worship Jesus Christ.

Yours, and Captivated.

Be Encouraged!

Treasuring Jesus Is Life Transforming

Unto you therefore which believe, He is precious.
2 Peter 2:7 KJV

Dear Family in Christ,

I have been asking the Lord lately just what He wants to see when He looks upon His Church:

"Lord Jesus, what is *Your* desire, *Your* vision for your Church?"

Increasingly, the impression upon my heart is being simplified, focused, and intensified:

The Lord's vision for us is that we be a people who treasure Him supremely.

Now, while this may not sound profound, it is profound, and in the most profound way. What could be more radical, powerful, and God-pleasing than treasuring Jesus Christ more than anything else? What could better honour the Father than treasuring His Son? What could produce a heart for holiness more surely than loving Jesus above all? What can motivate for mission more powerfully than a Christ-treasuring desire to see Him famous where today He is not?

Today there are no end of books available on "Vision" or "Strategy" or "Church Growth." They contain many valuable truths, and some of them are worthy of our attention. Seminars abound for Christians on "Leadership Dynamics" and "Mission Motivation." No doubt much can be gained by them ...

But what substitute can there ever be for a white-hot heart of love for Jesus? Should we not seek and cultivate such at all costs? Does He Himself not tell us that a heart hot with love for Jesus comes from a knowledge and experience of the depths of our forgiveness and deliverance from a deserved hell?

He who has been forgiven much, loves much.

I am convinced that a Church that truly *gets* the Gospel, understanding the depth and length and breadth and height of the love of Christ - amazed by the salvation of such ruined sinners as ourselves - will increasingly love and treasure Christ. Watch that church grow in holiness, and mission power!

It was JESUS - and nothing less - which captivated the Church in the New Testament:

I want to Know Christ! (Philippians 3:10)

For Christ's love compels us. (2 Corinthians 5:14)

For me to live is Christ! (Philippians 1:21)

Unto [us] who believe he is precious!(2 Peter 2:7 KJV)

I consider everything as loss compared to the surpassing greatness of knowing Christ. (Philippians 3:8)

God has poured out His love into our hearts. (Romans 5:5)

Let us fix our eyes on Jesus! (Hebrews 12:2)

Even so, come, Lord Jesus! (Revelation 22:20 KJV)

It was nothing less than Jesus Himself who captivated the hearts, minds, and lives of countless men and women of history who crossed continents, gave up comforts, challenged powers of darkness, and transformed their generations. I am challenged and blessed by the lives of the great Jesus-Lovers of Church history:

The Apostles, John, Peter, PaulThomas (the doubter, who took the Gospel all the way to India!) Polycarp (who was burned at the stake in the 2nd century),Amy Carmichael, William and Catherine Booth,John Wesley,George Whitefield,Corrie Ten-Boom, Loren Cunningham,Susannah Wesley,Jackie Pullinger, George Verwer.

OH! The list could go on and on! How about adding *your name* to that list?

Beloved, may we be a Jesus-loving people. That will solve no end of problems and give us sure focus, joy, purpose, and direction.

If you are going to so cultivate your heart, I urge you to get into the Bible, get on your knees (and face!) and ask God the Holy Spirit to reveal Jesus to you in the Book that He breathed.

May we be known as people who Love, Treasure, and Value the Lord Jesus above all the world.

Yours Treasuring Him.

Be Encouraged!

The Captive of Christ is the Freest Man on Earth

For in the gospel the righteousness of God is revealed, a righteousness that is by faith from first to last, just as it is written: "The righteous will live by faith."
Romans1:17

Friends,

In April of 1521, a little German monk stood before the most powerful council of the times.

As Martin Luther addressed the Pope's representatives, having been called to account for the challenges which he had made regarding some of the practices of the Church in his day, how his heart must have raced!

Luther's concern was for the Gospel. In particular, he was concerned that it be made clear that a person was put right with God, not by the efforts of man, or by the decree of the Church, but by simple reliance upon the death of Christ upon the Cross as a right payment for his sins. The keystone for Martin Luther was the doctrine of "Justification by grace alone, through faith alone." That is: a conviction from the Bible that salvation comes solely from the undeserved favour of God, and is secured by the individual solely through faith in Christ's death for his sins.

Now, this Truth, although plainly taught in the Bible, made the Pope and his Cardinals very angry. They had actually been *selling* salvation to masses of people, promising them and their loved ones release from Purgatory through the payment of money. The slogan was:

When a coin in the coffer rings, a soul from Purgatory springs.

Martin Luther's brave challenge was actually a threat to the money-making machine that was the mediaeval Church.

Luther became a hunted man!

The Pope summoned Luther to his representative council and demanded that Luther withdraw his assertion that salvation was by grace through faith alone, and fall into line with the established church. Luther stood alone before the greatest power on earth!

Before the Papal representative, Martin Luther, the brave monk from Wittenberg, made the following declaration which I personally believe was and is the single most profound statement made in the last 500 years.

> *Unless I am convinced by proofs from Scripture, or by plain and clear reason and arguments, I can and will not retract. For my conscience is held captive to the Word of God and it is neither safe nor wise to do anything against conscience. Here I stand. I can do no other. God Help Me! Amen.*

Now, I believe that this moment, when Luther proclaimed before the Papal Council that his mind and his conscience were gripped, "held captive" by the Bible, that Luther was in fact the freest man in all of Europe. I think it was the historian Thomas Carlyle who observed that this very same moment was the moment in which Freedom was birthed in Europe, (I am quite sure that I read this of Carlyle years ago ... but I cannot find the exact quote again!).

Just what was so profound about this statement from Luther? Why do I say that it was the most profound statement of the last 500 years? Why can April 1521 be seen as the birthday of the freedoms we so take for granted in our day?

Well, picture the scene: A pudgy little monk is bravely standing before the Pope's representative. The Pope is the most powerful man in all Europe, if not the world. He owns not just lands and buildings, *he owns people's thoughts.* There is no freedom to think what the Pope tells you not to think. He alone, from his papal office, can declare what one should believe. He alone can interpret the Bible. He alone has the very keys to Heaven!

But! The little monk has been *reading* the Bible. He has discovered therein Jesus Christ and His Gospel. His heart has been set free by Truth! His conscience has been captured by the Love of Christ! What he has discovered in the Bible is revolutionary:

Jesus Christ and His Gospel set people Free: Free to think, free to explore, free to govern their own souls before a holy God.

Indeed, the freest person on earth is the slave of Christ and His Gospel! There is perhaps no more powerful Truth. It is dynamite. Jesus said: *"... you will know the Truth, and the Truth will set you free."* (John 8:32)

That is why it is imperative that we be Bible People. That is why it is non-negotiable that the Bible *and Bible teaching* be at the centre of the Church. That is why we, each of us, need to be Bible readers and lovers of Truth.

Here is why Satan will do all that he can to get you, your family, a Church, a nation to marginalize the Scriptures and replace what God has said with what man thinks.

Beloved, we must be - now and always - Bible-people. As Wesley said, "A people of the Book." Read it. Believe it. Make your pastor preach it. Love it. Be transformed and set free by it.

Yours, Being Transformed.

Be Encouraged!

Stuff or Spirit: It is One or the Other

In Him was Life, and that Life was the Light of Men.
John 1:4

Dear Follower,

How does one know just what is final, ultimate Truth? When you boil it down, there are not very many options available.Really, there are only two alternatives.The first is that *matter*, by that I mean *stuff*, is eternal.The second is that *spirit*, by that I mean *something other than* stuff, is eternal. There really are no other options offered. Either Stuff is eternal, or Spirit is.

Now, the "Materialist" believes that Stuff has always, in one form or another, existed. Matter just *is*. He cannot explain from where it came. He may say that at one time it was all compressed into a very tiny, very dense ball which blew up and in time made the universe as we know it. But it always existed. This is what atheists believe to be ultimately True.

The "Spiritualist" (I am using this word merely to describe the person who believes in God, not in the spooky sense) believes that Spirit, or a Spirit, has always existed. He, like the Materialist, cannot explain where Spirit came from. When asked by the Materialist: "Who made God?" he shrugs and says "I have no way of answering that question, for God has always been," just as the Materialist shrugs when asked: "Where did stuff come from?" and says "I cannot answer that, for Stuff has always been."

So, the Materialist *believes* in Stuff; the Spiritualist *believes* in Spirit. Both are *believers*!

Now, to any reasonable mind, one of the two options (and remember, there really are no others) must be false and the other True.

When you think back through history, and imagine back to the very, very beginning of everything (something which we really cannot do), you come to a place where either Stuff or Spirit was there first.

The Bible says that Spirit was there first. It's very opening words boldly proclaim:

In the Beginning God. (Genesis 1:1)

Likewise, the first century fisherman, John, the son of a man named Zebedee, the business partner of a tough guy named Peter, who walked with Jesus, says that Sprit was first:

In the Beginning was the Word ... without Him nothing was made that has been made ... The Word became flesh and made His dwelling among us ... (John 1:1,3,14)

In Him was Life and the Life was the light of men ... (John 1:4)

It is the teaching of the Bible that God, Spirit, was first, and that later on He made Stuff. Stuff owes its existence to Spirit.

It is the teaching of the Atheist that Stuff was first, somehow became intelligent, and invented the idea of God.

The conviction of the Bible is that the Spirit became a man, and that everything that exists was made by the first century carpenter from Nazareth, Jesus Christ:

For by Him all things were created, in heaven and on earth visible and invisible. (Colossians 1:16)

One of these options is right, and one is wrong.

Now, I believe that the Bible's claim matches the two great questions - which relentlessly present themselves to all of us - better than does the Materialist's claim:

"Why is the Universe, in its amazing order, *here* instead of *not here?*"

And:

"Why am *I* here, and *aware* that I am here?"

These two questions are huge. I believe that Christians can give better answers to these two questions than Materialists can. We cannot give perfect answers, for in the end these are deep mysteries, but we can give better answers.

The Atheist can only say: "It is all by chance and ultimately has no meaning." That is a very convenient answer when one wants to not play fair, or cheat on his wife, or wipe out a people group, but it in the end leaves one empty.

The Christian can only say: "We, and all else, are here by the design of a loving God." That, at times, can be a very inconvenient answer, but I am discovering that it is taking me down a road which is growing increasingly colourful and purposeful. As challenging as this answer inevitably is to my selfishness, it better matches the evidence of the world around me and the cry of the heart within me.

Atheism just will not do. In the end, it does not make sense and leaves one in a cold, silent universe.

Belief in God may leave me with many unanswered questions, but it does not leave me finally in an empty universe. And, of all the "Spiritualist" options out there (and there are basically four, which you can explore for yourself: Pantheist, Dualist, Deist, Theist (of which there are basically three: Muslim, Jewish, and Christian). Christianity goes further, and is richer than all the others, and is, I believe the **Truth.** Besides, it is the only one whose founder is called "the Friend of Sinners."

No matter how hard it may sometimes be, no matter what questions remain - for now - unresolved, I (gladly) see no option but to embrace the Christian witness to Jesus as the Truth.

Yours In Jesus.

Be Encouraged!

There is No Hiding Behind Questions

What is Truth?
John 18:38

The above question was asked by a cynical Pontius Pilate directly to Jesus, as Jesus, bound and on trial, stood before him.

But it was not a serious question, and Pilate was not looking for any serious answers.

Pilate was hiding behind the question.

Questions can be convenient. Answers can be inconvenient ... Very inconvenient.

Pilate would have made a great poster-child for our times. People today are happy to hide behind their supposed inability to find "Truth." We like to pretend that we are earnest Truth seekers, and that the Truth is so hard to find. We post-modern people portray ourselves as "looking for God" or "Meaning" or "Truth" and "God/Meaning/ Truth" as off somewhere playing hide and seek.

Jesus just does not take the bait. He does not feel sorry for us "Truth seekers." He does not see the human race as a group of basically honest folk who would follow the Truth if only they could just find it. In fact, all through the Bible, it is not we poor people who do the looking for the hiding God, but it is God who, in grace and mercy, does the looking for the wicked, sinful, HIDING people!

It was Adam and Eve who hid. God did the looking. It is the sheep who wanders off. The shepherd looks. It is the coin that is lost. The woman looks. It is the rebel son who runs. The father waits, looking.

The problem is not God. He is not hard to find. He is looking! The problem is people. We love sin more than Truth, and so we come up with pitiful excuses that we "just cannot find God" and that we "cannot find truth," as if *they* were doing the hiding!

Truth inconveniences those of us who would rather sin than follow Jesus. Answers would flush us out of hiding and into the light, where we would have no more excuses for our bad behaviour.

Jesus had just said to Pilate: "Everyone who is on the side of Truth listens to me." (v 38). That is a bold statement, but what Jesus was declaring most emphatically was that anyone who earnestly wants to *get right with God* will have no trouble seeing Jesus as the way to do just that.

Elsewhere Jesus said plainly that we refuse to believe, because we are more concerned with what people think of us than with what God thinks of us:

How can you believe if you accept praise from one another, but make no effort to obtain praise that comes from God? (John 5:44)

Still again Jesus plainly stated that unbelief is rooted in our own love of sin: "Light has come into the world, but men loved darkness instead of the light because their deeds were evil. Everyone who does evil hates the light and will not come into the light for fear that his deeds will be exposed." (John 3:19,20)

Jesus boldly claimed:

I am the Light of the World. Whoever follows me will not walk in darkness [ignorance] *but will have the Light of life.* (John 8:12)

Beloved, there is no problem with God. It is not He who is ducking around corners, afraid of being found. He has revealed Himself in the very world around us finally and Truly in Jesus Christ. Had Pilate asked his question, "What is Truth?" in an earnest manner, he would have seen that Truth was standing right in front of Him in the person of Jesus. As it was, his question was an evasion, a stiff-arm, not an earnest plea, but flippant mock. It was a "leaning back in the chair, feet on the desk" type of question.

Jesus Christ is "The Truth" (John 14:6). He will inconvenience you, flush you out of the dingy corners where you are hiding, and give you answers which will leave you no choice but to repent of your sin and follow Him, or turn aside and perish. In the end, if you will have it, He will grant you Life in all its Fullness.

Knowing Him is worth it all.

Grace and Peace.

Be Encouraged!

Our Confidence is Rooted in Christ, Not in Ourselves

For it is we ... who put no confidence in the flesh ...
Philippians 3:3

Friends,

"Buttock Implants Could Improve Your Confidence"

No, I have not lost my mind.

That was headline news recently on one of the Internet news pages.

The story was of some famous actress (of whom I have never heard), whose life has been transformed, right down to the level of her very confidence, by her recent "buttock implants."

Clearly, she had put a whole new light on the ancient command to "not covet your neighbour's ass." (Exodus 20:17) (Sorry... that was irresistible ...)

Now, I have never heard of such devices. I really don't want to spend too much time considering the particulars of them (the imagination boggles). What I do want to consider is the tragedy of a culture, whose heroes and heroines can inspire us, lead us, motivate us toward such misplaced sources of confidence. Here is a case where a person's faith is literally in her backside. For others, their confidence may be in the particular phone they own, or the hairstyle they sport, or their cars, or stock portfolio.

How Trivial!

How Shallow!

How Damnable!

Here we are, the very pinnacle of God's Creation, made in His Image. Created to:

* Know Him.

* Worship him.

* Relate to Him.

And instead we become miserable little idolaters, whose role models must inject silicone into their backsides in order to feel better about themselves. Beloved, our "confidence" must come from Christ: His Person, His Work on the Cross, His victorious Resurrection.

We are to put no confidence in the flesh (Philippians 3:3). The Lord Himself is to be our confidence (Psalm 71:5).We can be confident that the Lord will complete what he has begun in us (Phil 1:6).

Even more, we can approach the throne of Grace with confidence (Hebrews 4:16). Because of Jesus we have confidence before God (1 John 3:21).

Beware of misplacing your confidence. Place it in Christ ALONE. And, as for implants, ask Him to implant His:

Joy,Hope,

Assurance, Victory

Deep within:

Where nothing can disturb.

Where no surgeon can ever cut.

Where no thief can ever steal.

Where Christ Alone can dwell.

We need to fight against the spirit of the age and its relentless attempts at incursions into our souls. We cannot allow such ceaseless efforts to erode the very image of God of which, among all Creation, we are the sole bearers.

Yours, Confident in Christ.

Be Encouraged!

Ten Prayers That God is Certain to Say "Yes!" To

This is the confidence we have in approaching God: that if we ask anything according to His will, He hears us.
1 John 5:14

1) That God will graciously cause you to be Supremely Delighted in Him.

Delight yourself in the Lord,
and he will give you the desires of your heart. (Psalm 37:4)

2) That the Love of Jesus, displayed in the Gospel, will satisfy you way down deep, at heart-level.

Satisfy us in the morning with your unfailing love,
that we may sing for joy and be glad all our days. (Psalm 90:14)

3) That you will be given grace to Treasure Christ above everything and everyone else.

Unto you therefore which believe he is precious ... (1 Peter2:7 KJV)

4) That you will be given a heart desire to grow in your Knowledge of Christ.

But grow in the grace and knowledge of our Lord and Saviour Jesus Christ. To him be glory both now and forever! Amen. (2 Peter 3:18)

5) That the Holy Spirit will open your heart and mind to understand the Scriptures.

I keep asking that the God of our Lord Jesus Christ, the glorious Father, may give you the Spirit of wisdom and revelation, so that you may know him better.

I pray that the eyes of your heart may be enlightened in order that you may know the hope to which he has called you, the riches of his glorious inheritance in his holy people, and his incomparably great power for us who believe. That power is the same as the mighty strength he exerted when he raised Christ from the dead and seated him at his right hand in the heavenly realms. (Ephesians 1:17-20)

6) That you will be given a Heart to Love others, because you know how much God loves you.

And this is my prayer: that your love may abound more and more in knowledge and depth of insight, so that you may be able to discern what is best and may be pure and blameless for the day of Christ, filled with the fruit of righteousness that comes through Jesus Christ – to the glory and praise of God. (Philippians 1:9-11)

7) That you will love the unbeliever and have a longing to see him saved.

For Christ's love compels us, because we are convinced that one died for all ... (2 Corinthians 5:14)

8) That God Himself will overwhelm you with Hope, so that you become a Source of Hope for Others.

May the God of hope fill you with all joy and peace as you trust in him, so that you may overflow with hope by the power of the Holy Spirit. (Romans 15:13)

9) That you will be given grace to count all things as nothing compared to knowing Christ.

What is more, I consider everything a loss because of the surpassing worth of knowing Christ Jesus my Lord, for whose sake I have lost all things. I consider them rubbish, that I may gain Christ ...
(Philippians 3:8)

10) That God will give you a supernatural spirit of expectancy and faith, to see Him work far beyond all that you can ask or imagine.

Now to him who is able to do immeasurably more than all we ask or imagine, according to his power that is at work within us ...
(Ephesians 3:20)

Yours, Praying in Faith.

Be Encouraged!

The Lord Is Eager to Bless You

May the Lord make you increase, both you and your children. May you be blessed by the Lord, The Maker of heaven and earth.
Psalm 115:14,15

The above passage blessed me during one of my quiet times with the Lord. I have often returned to it, just to meditate upon it and to encourage my soul. It is a passage of increase and blessing. It reveals the heart of God towards His children and His Church.

We do not worship a miserly God. He is abundant in His heart towards us. He longs to give:

... a good measure, pressed down, shaken together, and running over. (Luke 6:38).

It is from:

... the fullness of His grace that we have all received one blessing after another. (John 1:16)

for He is:

... for us ... (Romans 8:31) and not against us.

Now, until we *get this*, until we understand and receive this Truth regarding God's heart towards us, we will never make spiritual progress. We have been declared righteous in Christ. Indeed, God has made:

... Him who had no sin to be sin for us, so that in him we might become the righteousness of God. (2 Cor. 5:21)

It is because of the gift of Christ's righteousness, His very goodness credited to us, that God our Father has only good disposed towards us. It is not that God just "puts up with us", but that He welcomes us and receives us in Jesus Christ. For:

He who did not spare His own Son, but gave Him up for us all - how will He not also, along with Him, graciously give us all things?
(Romans 8:32)

There can be no greater tonic for the soul. This is the medicine that we need! God is "for us" in and through Jesus Christ. I do not know the depths of the battles which you are facing. I cannot imagine some of the trials going on within and around you just now. But I *know* that if you are a humble believer in Jesus, that God wants to increase His grace to you and to bless "both you and your children."

So, Battle on! "Be strong in the Lord, and the strength of His might." (Ephesians 6:10) Position yourself in the place of victory in Jesus, and keep praying, believing, warring for your children, your church, your community, your own heart, whatever the situation.

Yours, and ready to be blessed.

Be Encouraged!

The Lord Will Fill You With His Word For Your Good

My soul glorifies the Lord, and my spirit rejoices in God my Saviour.
Luke 1:46

So began Mary's Song.

Upon receiving the news that she was to be "highly favored" in bearing the very Son of God, this Godly girl broke forth into a hymn of praise which has for two millennia amazed theologians, inspired faithful believers, and moved the pens of poets like none other.

Let us take a few minutes and marvel at the holy heart of this teenager, that we might gain encouragement for our lives and come to our own place of self-surrender, echoing the heart, if not the words of Mary:

I am the Lord's Servant, May it be to me as you have said.   (Luke 1:38)

This girl *knew her Bible.* She had applied herself as a young woman to knowing the God of Truth. Her brief song, comprising a mere nine verses in our Bible, contains references to no less that eighteen Old Testament passages. Her short song draws from the Psalms, Isaiah, The Exodus, 2 Samuel, Jeremiah, and Habakkuk.

Truly, out of the abundance of both her mind and heart, her mouth was speaking! JC Ryle wrote of her:

Clearly, the Virgin Mary's mind was full of Scripture. So, when out of the fullness of her heart her mouth spoke, she uttered scriptural language ... She chose words which the Holy Spirit had already consecrated and used.

Think about this with me: Her young life had just experienced a *total* change in direction. God had come calling. Whatever *her* plans were, they were no more. Her goals were now swallowed up in God's greater purposes. And her response was:

Worshipful submission.

Now, such a response to the suddenness of God comes from one who has been walking with God, immersing oneself in God's Word. George Muller, who transformed so many in his Bristol orphanages wrote:

I believe that the one reason that I have been kept in happy useful service is that I have been a lover of Holy Scripture. It has been my habit to read the Bible through four times a year; in a prayerful spirit, to applyit to my heart, and practice what I find there. I have been for sixty-nine years a happy man; happy, happy, happy.

Mary was *ready* for the call of God upon her life. She clearly had not been spending her formative years goofing off. (I sadly fear that we today seem to believe that children and teenagers cannot be excellent in their walk with God. The Bible is full of examples of very young men and women who rebuke our unbelief in this area.) We have said often the truth that each and every one of us is as holy as we want to be. Mary wanted to be Godly. She set her life apart to be so and was ready when God knocked on the door of her heart.

I marvel that the God of Eternity chose not a queen, nor an heiress, but a poor girl with a pure heart.

Mary stands to instruct and inspire us. She rebukes our indolence and worldliness. She has been, and shall be for generations an example of what God can do with a humble, available life.

May she encourage us at Christmas, and year-round, toward consecrated living.

May our Lord Jesus Christ Himself and God our Father, who loved us and by His grace gave us eternal encouragement and good hope, encourage your hearts and strengthen you in every good deed and word. (2 Thessalonians 2:16-17)

Yours,For a Higher Purpose.

Be Encouraged!

Jesus Tells Us the Secret of Life

Whoever finds his life will lose it, and whoever loses his life for my sake will find it.
Matthew 10:39

Dear Friends,

An acquaintance of mine is currently in the process of having his gender changed. He is, at surface level, "becoming a woman." Currently he is wearing women's clothing and taking a range of hormone therapy. He is due soon to have an operation to make the change final.

Most of the people I know who know him, view him as a bit of a hero. They see him as being "true to himself." He has a wife and two children, so they see him as being "true to himself" at "great personal cost." It is really quite something to behold the accolades he receives.

Now, I like this bloke, finding him to be a friendly fellow. We have some interests in common and can engage readily in warm conversation. I think I do a good job at looking beyond his surface appearance (the mascara and such) and towards his heart. Furthermore, I believe I am pretty sensitive to whatever pain, trauma, and sin may have taken place in his life which has brought him to this place and to this decision. I can fairly say that I care about him.

But in fact, what he is doing is profoundly selfish. While he is my friend, I do not look upon him as a hero.

What he is doing really sums up the spirit of our age. It demands that I be "true to myself" no matter what. It screams that I have a "right to happiness," no matter what pain I may inflict upon others in my pursuit of that happiness.

One was once considered noble who, no matter at what cost to himself, was faithful to his vows, duty, and what was right. Now one is considered so who pursues his dream no matter what it may cost others. Sportsmen who win championships at the expense of their families are now "brave," and couples are deemed "heroic" when they make the "hard choice" to abort their child for the sake of their careers or lifestyles.

Now this spirit is exactly the opposite of the Spirit that was in Christ. It is diametrically opposed to the call of Christ to a life of discipleship. This modern spirit refuses to deal with the fact that my "self" is flawed by sin and polluted. It closes its eyes to the fact that *I* am what is wrong with the world, and that Christ is not calling me to "fulfill" myself, but to deny myself.

To put it bluntly, if I were "true to myself" as a life-principle, I would probably be divorced, bankrupt, and in prison by now. My "self" is my problem.

Look at the words of Jesus at the top of this page. They are foundational to Christian living. They are cognizant of a sinful nature, and of the need for Christ to impart new life in the heart. They are revolutionary.

They warn me and my confused friend that life is not found by seeking self-fulfillment, but by radically denying sinful self and treasuring Christ above what I see as my "rights" and "privileges." But right here is where Jesus makes all the difference and provides the miracle. For even as we say "no" to our self-will, God is saying "Yes," a Divine "Yes," to His greater Will for us. It is as we lay down our lives, that He raises up our lives and imparts His Divine "Life" to us. He aims not to extinguish, but to inflame us. The Christian understanding of denying self is not in the same category as, say, the Hindu view of "extinguishing" all desire. It is not our goal to desire "nothing," but "something," that being, to know Jesus and to become all that He has purposed us to be.

C.S. Lewis rightly observed that it is when I turn to Christ, when I give myself up to His Personality that I first begin to have a real personality of my own ... Look within yourself, and you will find in the long run only hatred, loneliness, despair, rage, ruin and decay. But look to Christ and you will find Him, and with Him, everything else!

My concern for my friend is that when he "discovers himself" he will findsomeone he still does not like ... a broken-hearted soul in need of a much deeper cure than a surgeon's knife and some hormones can offer. Perhaps then, through all the heartache and tears cried in the battle over self, he will find Life in losing his life, for the sake of Christ and others (wife and children).

I know that's the old-fashioned way, but it is also the way of the Kingdom which is coming.

Yours for Christ, His Gospel and His Kingdom.

Be Encouraged!

If Sin Leads to Death, Then Holiness Leads to Life!

And sin, when it is full-grown, gives birth to death.
James 1:15

Dear Family in Christ,

I have been meditating upon the tragic life of Saul, Israel's first king. How telling it is to trace the development of sin in that miserable man's life!

I am sure that he, as a younger man, never once imagined that he could get as entrapped in sin as he finally did. The little jealousies and duplicities in his heart grew until they consumed his very life.

I don't think that we realize just how dangerous and wicked sin is, especially in regard to our own sins. It will do us good to contemplate and consider the growth of sin in a soul. We should view the least trace of it with a greater horror than we would a cancer. (If we were as afraid of diseases of the soul as we are of those of the body we would be better, holier, happier followers of Jesus.)

The scripture above warns us that sin *grows*. It does not stay put. It metastasizes, just as a vicious cancer will. It is not content to occupy a corner of one's life. It wants to kill and destroy its victim.

We simply do not take sin seriously enough. We never imagine that it will *ruin* us.

We put up with tumors of pride, jealousy, lust and greed, never considering that they will spread throughout our entire souls.

We think we can control sin, and keep it under locks, allowing it out on occasion for our enjoyments.

But it GROWS....

And when fully grown, it brings forth DEATH - soul death, bodily death, relational death, eternal death.

It is not funny and is nothing to joke about.

It is especially horrid when considered in the light of the value of the soul which it destroys, the God which it dishonours, and the Divine Image which it defaces.

I want to encourage you to do three things:

First, make it a regular part of your prayer life to ask God to help you see the sin in your life the way He sees it. Get serious about this. Be as serious with your soul as you are with your body, and more so. Ask the Lord to give you a real revelation of the horror of sin, death, and hell. Don't allow yourself to go soft on this!

Then, ask the Lord to help you understand in an ever new and deepening way, just what it means to repent before the Cross and receive cleansing through the Blood of Jesus. His death for our sins is sufficient to cleanse and restore the sin-sick soul. What joy and release there is when Christ cleanses sin! I believe that we can shout "hallelujah!" when we truly experience the cleansing blood of Christ.

Finally, meditate upon the beauty of holiness. A life which is being conformed to the image of Christ is an increasingly beautiful life. The soul becomes rich and healthy, God is honored, and the Image of God shines through the redeemed person's life. Holiness is a colorful, life-giving, rich state of life which should be cherished and pursued at all costs!

Indeed, if sin, when full-grown, gives birth to death, then godliness gives birth to Life!

May we receive the grace God is offering to take sin seriously, believe in the Blood of Christ shed for us earnestly, and pursue holiness passionately.

Yours, For the Beauty of Life in Christ.

Be Encouraged!

You Cannot Lose When Trusting in the Lord

It is better to take refuge in the LORD than to trust in princes.
Psalm 118:9

Friend,

How could it ever be better to trust in the Invisible than in the visible? How could it ever be better to trust in the Lord, whom you cannot see, and in whose Word alone you must plant your flag of faith, than in a man, a great prince, whom you can see, and whose wealth and power are plainly evident before your eyes?

Imagine that a great prince was your friend. Imagine that he took a special interest in you. How many doors would fling open for *you* because of *him*? How many opportunities would be available to *you* because of your favored position with your princely friend?How many deliverances would be *yours* because of the power of *his* word? Just imagine your sense of security and privilege!

Certainly such a friendship would inspire you toward:

* attempting the otherwise impossible,

*living a life which displayed the value which you placed in your princely friend,

*speaking of his goodness and spreading his fame everywhere.

Trusting in a prince would provide you with security, influence, wealth, favour, opportunity, and prestige.

Unless ... The prince changed his mind about you. Or you disappointed him. Or he underwent a change in character. Or someone bigger than that prince deposed your friendly monarch, someone who had no regard for you. (Indeed! The new man might

---

204

even cut your head off seeing that you were friendly with the old regime!)

Trusting in princes is fine when all is well. But times change. Circumstances change. Princes change.

Actually, you can take the word "princes" out, and substitute any range of words:

*Money

*Health

*Job

*Friends

*Family

None of these is necessarily evil. But none is capable of providing ultimate security. They finally must, and will, all fail you.

So, our Psalmist informs us from personal experience, that it is actually better to take refuge, that is trust in the Invisible God, than in even the greatest, most powerful visible thing (a prince) imaginable.

Why? What is it about the Lord that makes Him a better hope than the best the world has to offer? Just consider the following with me:

*The Lord is Everlasting. A prince is temporary. (Psalm 90:2)

*The Lord is Unchanging. A prince is sure to change. (Hebrews 13:8)

*The Lord is perfect in His Holiness. A prince is a sinner. (Psalm 22:3)

*The Lord is perfect in His Judgments. A prince is sure to make mistakes. (Romans11:33)

*The Lord is rich in Mercy. A prince will run out of patience. (2 Samuel 24:14)

*The Lord brings all things to good. A prince has no such power. (Romans 8:28)

*The Lord will never leave a child in shame. A prince may prove to have been a foolish one in whom to place one's trust. (Psalm 25)

*The Lord is Sovereign and cannot be deposed. A prince can be taken down in a moment. (Revelation 17:14)

*The Lord will never leave you or forsake you. A prince will someday let you down. (Hebrews 13:5)

*The Lord understands all our weaknesses. A prince simply cannot. (Psalm 103:14)

*The Lord understands our temptations and helps us. A prince simply cannot. (Hebrews 4:15)

*The Lord will never weary of our coming. A prince can get exasperated. (Luke 18:1-8)

*The Lord is an inexhaustible source of Grace. A prince has a short supply. (John 1:16)

*The Lord is close to the broken-hearted, and He saves those who are crushed in spirit. A prince wants strong people around him. (Psalm 34:18)

*The Lord strengthens the weary. A prince wearies his subjects. (Psalm 29:11)

*The Lord can do the impossible. A prince cannot always even do the possible. (Jeremiah 32:17)

*The Lord gives His Life for His enemies. A prince's friends give their lives for him. (Romans 5:8)

*The Lord grants forgiveness of sin and Eternal Life to undeserving sinners. A prince has no such prerogative. (Romans 4:5)

*The Lord knows what is best for you and is shaping all events for your good and His glory. A prince cares not finally about any good but his own. (Romans 8:28-39)

*The Lord has conquered death and grants Life and Immortality to all who trust in Him. A prince will die and decay in the ground. (2 Timothy 1:10)

*The Lord is the Judge of all men, including princes. A prince will give an account to the Lord. (2 Corinthians 5:10)

Indeed! It *is* better to take refuge in the Lord, than to trust in princes!

Thankful for Jesus and counting on Him.

Be Encouraged!

Here is a Key to Thankfulness

In everything give thanks, for this is God's will for you in Christ Jesus.
1 Thessalonians 5:18

Dear Family in Christ,

I want to write a simple word for us, that we may be encouraged and challenged to be truly thankful people.

As the Apostle Paul wrote the Thessalonians, he was urging them to "rejoice evermore, pray without ceasing, and give thanks in all circumstances," reminding them that this in fact was "God's will for them in Christ Jesus."

How could he urge them (and us) to be always thankful? Were there not, and are there not, endless things to rob them, and us, of reasons to be thankful? Is such an injunction not just "positive thinking," "whistling in the rain," "pretending?"

Not for the Apostle. Nor should it be for us.

He was a man who was always thinking from the greater to the lesser. For Him, the great issue of life had been solved. He had been saved from sin through the Lord Jesus and given the gift of Eternal Life! God's wrath had been carried away through the sufferings of Jesus, and the very righteousness of Christ had been applied to him.

All this was by grace and guaranteed by Christ's blood.

Here, for Paul, was the basis for a thankful heart. Here was his reason for joy in all circumstances. Here was his encouragement to pray continually and not give way to a bitter, complaining spirit.

So it is for us. Through the Lord Jesus and His atoning death and victorious resurrection *all the big issues have been dealt with*

208

and secured. We are Saved and Safe forever. We have begun a journey with Jesus into eternity which will grow ever brighter and brighter.

Now, we can approach all other issues and trials from a great place of salvation and security. How can we be anything but thankful people when we consider the greatness of our salvation that allows us to live life in light of the Gospel? Certainly trials, even those of the most severe nature, take on a different hue when the light of the Gospel and of Salvation is displayed upon them.

I, for one, can forget so quickly to be thankful in every circumstance. But I need to remember to live in the light of my salvation. In that light, I can see that every trial is intended to press me closer to my beloved Jesus, wean me from this world as a source of joy, and fit me for the Eternity of which I am an heir.

May we be truly thankful people. Thankful for the Glorious Gospel of Jesus Christ. Thankful for the thousands of daily mercies which the Lord sends our way. Thankful for the trials which press us upon the Lord Jesus.

Make a list today of as many blessings for which you can give thanks. Make sure you put "Salvation" at the top.

Yours, Thankfully.

Be Encouraged!

God Invites Us to Share in His Holiness

... and Pursue Holiness ...
Hebrews 12:14

Dear Brothers and Sisters,

I want to spur you on today in your walk with Jesus. The above three words, taken from the Letter to the Hebrews (12:14), are packed with purpose and meaning. They are aggressive, not passive. They are goal-oriented and therefore life-shaping. They rebuke laziness and award diligence.

These words speak of a goal: Holiness. Please do not cringe at this word! It is a beautiful word. Holiness describes the Lord in His very essence. He is utterly pure. He contains nothing which is tainted. He has never had a bad thought or dream, never pronounced an evil word or performed a sinful deed. He is good to the core of His being, always has been and always shall be.

He is Holy. His holiness is beautiful and renders Him worthy of all our worship.

Now, God possesses certain attributes which are His and His alone. We will never, in any measure possess these attributes. I am speaking here of His Eternality, His Omniscience (all-knowing), Omnipresence (everywhere present), and His Omnipotence (all-powerful). These attributes are His, alone.

But God possesses other attributes which to one degree or another He deigns to share with us. I am speaking here of things such as His Love, Mercy, Wisdom, and Justice. His Holiness is just such an attribute. The Eternal God desires to make us like Himself in His Holiness. Embrace this. Holiness is not a curse, but a blessing. Holiness, that is, true goodness at heart level, is a beautiful thing! In varying degrees, God in His grace can make us more loving, merciful, wise, just, and holy.

You can describe growth in Holiness simply as "becoming more and more like Jesus."

Now, our Bible verse at the top tells us that we have a part to play in our growth in holiness. We have to cooperate with God in this. Our pursuit of holiness is different in this regard than our initial salvation. When we are first saved from the guilt and penalty of our sin, we come to Jesus with no works of our own to offer. We receive pardon by the merits of Jesus and His death on the cross for our sins. He takes away our sin and gives us His righteousness in its place.

But to become more and more like Jesus, to grow in holiness, we must cooperate.

We "pursue" holiness. Like a boy pursues a girl, an athlete a prize, or a person pursues a dream, a Christian pursues becoming more like Jesus. He becomes increasingly consumed by this. He thinks about it, works on it, strategizes for it.

Becoming more like Jesus will not happen by accident. More so, the true Christian is distinguished from the false by his earnest desire to have done with the old ways and live a new way. I think it fair to say that if one does not want to become more like Jesus, that is, to grow in holiness, then he is most probably not His. In other words, one's salvation is proven - demonstrated - by one's pursuit of holiness.

Look, we are not saved by works. We are saved by grace, through faith alone. But we are saved to *become*. We are saved *to* as well as *from*. *From* sin, *to* Christ. And God is able and willing to give us all the grace we need to:

Battle heart and life sins. Seek Him in prayer. Discover Him in His Word. Put off the "old" and put on the "new." Growing in holiness requires spiritual effort and commitment. It is a *pursuit*, not just an automatic. And the results, the prize at the end, is a character that is larger for God, shaped like Christ, happy in Jesus.

Nobody will ever be sorry for pursuing holiness. Many will be sorry for not.

May we receive all the grace available to join in the magnificent obsession of becoming like Jesus!

Yours for Christ and forever.

Be Encouraged!

There is Power in a Thankful Heart

Do everything without complaining or arguing, so that you may become blameless and pure, children of God without fault in a crooked and depraved generation, in which you shine like stars in the universe as you hold out the Word of Life.
Philippians 2:14

Brothers and Sisters,

"Do everything without complaining," says the Apostle Paul to the believers in Philippi. Apparently there were believers in that church who had bad attitudes and would rather moan than be grateful. What a tragedy to the witness of Jesus is a complaining Christian and a complaining church!

Now it is always easy to take on board a complaining spirit. There are some who will simply not obey the Bible when it counsels us to be thankful people.

To be a complainer is sinful, especially in light of the wonders and greatness of God's mercy and grace. Yet some of us are undisciplined in our attitudes and have given ourselves over to a complaining spirit. For some, nothing is ever good enough!

How can Heaven-bound people, redeemed from sin and hell by Jesus' blood, become moaners and groaners? How dare a believer be anything less than generous in attitude and overflowing in thankfulness!

Well, I could easily complain in this letter about complaining and complainers! But I would rather extol the opposite spirit of thankfulness. I think that this will be more beneficial to us all, and may serve to sever the root of complaining which grows among us.

Below are six positive results of thankfulness. If you prefer to "go negative", just flip them on their heads and you will see six destructive results of complaining.

213

1) Thankfulness honours God by magnifying His goodness to us. A thankful spirit says "God you are good and are good to me." (Think about what a complaining spirit implies about God....)

You are my God and I will give you thanks; You are my God and I will exalt you. (Psalm 118:28)

2) Thankfulness lifts the eyes of one's heart above the mundane and unto the Heavens, and beyond the temporary to the Eternal. (Where does a complaining spirit fixate?)

O Lord, Our Lord! How majestic is Your Name in all the earth! You have set your glory above the heavens! (Psalm 8:1)

3) Thankfulness revives one's spirit, drives away despair, and changes one's life even if circumstances don't change. (Consider what a complaining heart does to one's spirit.)

... the cheerful heart has a continual feast. (Proverbs 15:15)

4) Thankfulness encourages you, *and* the believers around you and lifts up the heads of the weary. Thankfulness is contagious and healing to all around. (What poison might a complainer spread to those around him?)

A cheerful heart is good medicine. (Proverbs 17:22)

5) Thankfulness honours God's providential care and says "Lord, You are wise in all Your ways, and You are enough for me." (What does complaining say about God?)

... give thanks in all circumstances for this is the will of God for you In Christ Jesus. (1 Thessalonians 5:18)

6) Thankfulness enhances and beautifies the witness of the People of God in the world. (Ponder how complaining "uglifies" our witness to the world.)

... so that you may become blameless and pure, children of God without fault in a crooked and depraved generation, inwhich you

shine like stars in the universe as you hold out the Word of Life.
(Philippians 2:14)

We could go on and on! But perhaps the above is enough to encourage us all to repent of childish complaining, and discipline ourselves to be thankful people.

Yours, with a thankful heart.

Be Encouraged!

There is None Greater Than Jesus Christ

Now unto you therefore who believe, He is precious.
1 Peter 2:7 KJV

Henry Scougal (1650 - 1678) was a Scottish pastor and theologian. He lived a very short, but profoundly significant life. He left the world with a book *The Life of God in the Soul of Man,* a work as brief as was his life, but one which has gone on to influence millions of believers across the centuries and across the world. Indeed, the great George Whitefield said that he never really understood Christianity until he read that book.

The theme of the book can be summed up in one great sentence, which expresses one great idea:

The health of a soul is determined by the value of what it loves the most.

Just take a moment to consider that truth. You have a soul. It can be to one degree or another healthy or sickly. Many have mortally ill souls. Some have fit and healthy souls. Scougal's right-on observation was that the determining factor here is the object of the soul's affection. If you supremely love base and low things, your soul will suffer. If you supremely love noble things, your soul will be fit and well.

If you love that which is most precious and wonderful of all, then your soul will be truly well and full of life. The most wonderful and precious "thing" that there is, is none other than Jesus Christ. If He is rightly the object of your affections, then you will prosper, right down to your inner-being, even unto Eternal Life.

Jesus alone is worthy of our highest thoughts, our greatest efforts, and our deepest love.

Why? What is it about Jesus Christ that makes Him so wonderful and so worthy? Why is it tragic to attempt to love anything in the place of Jesus? Why should it be that Christians Treasure Him supremely, even more than life itself?

Why is Jesus "Precious" unto those who believe? It all has to do with two things:1) Who He *is* (His *person*). 2) What He *has done, is doing, and will do* (His *work*).

As for Who He Is, there is simply none like Him. The Bible says of Jesus:

He is the image of the invisible God, the firstborn over all creation. For by Him all things were created: things in heaven and on earth, visible and invisible, whether thrones or powers or rulers, or authorities, all things were created by Him and for Him. He is before all things and in Him all things hold together. And He is the head of the body, the Church, He is the beginning and the firstborn from among the dead, so that in everything He might have the supremacy. For God was pleased to have all His fullness dwell in Him, and through Him to reconcile to Himself all things, whether things on earth or in heaven, by making peace through His blood, shed on the cross.(Colossians 1: 15-20)

Now, it is *impossible* to think of or imagine a greater being than the one just described. Try to. Try as hard as you can. You cannot. Jesus Christ is superlative in every category. He is God the Son, one with the Father and the Spirit. Eternal, having no beginning or ending, He is the Creator and Sustainer and Redeemer of all.

The Apostle Paul, a man who was captivated and gripped by Christ, goes on to say of Him that in Christ:

... are hidden all the treasures of wisdom and knowledge.
(Colossians 2:3)

Imagine that! All learning, wisdom, science, discovery, beauty, intelligence, are somehow begun in none other than the Carpenter from Nazareth!

Knowing Him is the highest thing your mind can pursue. Loving Him is the very highest affection your heart can have. History has known many great men and women - some of them good, some of them wicked. Line them all up. Survey the great figures of history. You will not find Jesus Christ among them. He stands alone. He is in a different category. He is the Man who is God, the God who is Man. He is the Lord of History, the Judge of all, and the Saviour of Sinners.

He is precious because of Who He *Is*. But, if that were not enough, He is yet more precious for What He *has done, is doing, and will do.*This Eternal Creator God:

1) Became a Human Being. He really did. As Charles Wesley said, He "emptied Himself of all but love;" "Our God contracted to a span, incomprehensibly made man."

Who, being in the form of God, thought it not robbery to be equal with God:

But made himself of no reputation, and took upon him the form of a servant, and was made in the likeness of men:

And being found in fashion as a man, he humbled himself, and became obedient unto death, even the death of the cross.
(Philippians 2: 6-8 KJV)

Jesus was God walking on earth. He loved the loveless, rebuked the proud, cleansed the filthy, fed the hungry, touched the untouchable, healed the sick, rebuked the storms of nature, defied the devil, and raised the dead. He was Truth in human form.

2) Died a sacrificial death as a perfect Substitute for the sins of the world.

God made Him who knew no sin to be a sin-offering for us.
(2 Corinthians 5:21)

...and became obedient to death - even death on a cross.
(Philippians 2:8)

Wonder of Wonders! Jesus Christ gave " His life as a ransom for many." Every religion on the earth grapples with the problem of sin and the human heart. But it is Christ who came to bear sin, to offer Himself for sin, to deliver from sin, to pay for sin, to forgive sin.

3) Rose again in a Glorified Body, thus conquering death itself.

Therefore God exalted Him to the highest place... (Philippians 2:9)

... but God raised Him from the dead, freeing Him from the agony of death, because it was impossible for death to keep its hold on Him.
(Acts 2:24)

The grave did not have the final say over Jesus, and it will not have the final say over those who trust in Him! Indeed, as the hymnist said, "Vain the stone, the watch, the seal." People of every culture and time dread death. But death has been soundly defeated in Jesus and His resurrection. Visit all the tombs of the great and powerful, the graves of the weak and small. There is an empty tomb and a vacant grave where Jesus Christ is concerned.

4) Ascended into Heaven and grants forgiveness of sin and Life Eternal to all who trust in Him. He owns *all authority* in the entire Universe.

All authority in heaven and on earth has been given to me ...
(Matthew 28:18)

Salvation is found in no one else, for there is no other name under heaven given to men by which we must be saved. (Acts 4:12)

Jesus Christ will hear you when you pray. He lives today and is our way to the Father. The work He did once on the Cross, still speaks a word on our behalf before the very Throne of God. The way to the Father, to Heaven, to Life, is open for all who will come to Christ.

5) Is the final Judge of all men, and is King of Kings and Lord of Lords.

For He has set a day when He will judge the world with justice by the man [Jesus Christ] He has appointed. (Acts 17: 31)

All Creation has a date set ... an appointment ... with Jesus Christ. All will appear before His Judgment seat. There is no avoiding Him. He will sort out the tangles of history. He will make sense of it all. He will reign in justice and power. He will save those who tremble and believe, and punish those who refuse. Amazing Jesus Christ!

6) Is the Theme of Heaven and, together with the Father and the Holy Spirit, is the praise of all Redeemed Creation forever.

I did not see a temple in the city, because the Lord God Almighty and the Lamb are its temple. The city does not need the sun or the moon to shine on it, for the Glory of God gives it light, and the Lamb is its lamp. (Revelation 21:22)

Will you be bored in Heaven? Not if Christ is your Treasure, for He is the very theme and focus of Eternity. He wants all that the Father has given Him to be with Him and to behold His unfathomable Glory.

None can compare with the matchless Jesus Christ. Those who treasure Him supremely have, with healthy souls, lived to transform nations, families, homes, cultures. They have righted wrongs and turned what is upside-down right way up. They have loved the loveless and lived lives of significance and purpose.

May the Lord Jesus Himself be the delight of our souls, the chief aim of our affections, the "Pearl of Great Price," precious beyond all else to us.

Yours, to treasure Christ.

Why I follow Jesus

BECAUSE HE LOVES ME EVEN WHEN I DO NOT
    LOVE HIM
BECAUSE HE WILL NEVER LEAVE ME OR FORSAKE
    ME
BECAUSE HE BORE ALL MY SINS AWAY ON THE
    CROSS
BECAUSE HE ALONE HAS THE WORDS OF ETERNAL
    LIFE
BECAUSE HE PROMISES TO FINISH WHAT HE
    BEGAN IN ME
BECAUSE HE IS WONDERFUL
BECAUSE HE IS MERCIFUL
BECAUSE HE IS LORD
BECAUSE HE STANDS ALONE AMONG ALL THE
    GREATS OF HISTORY
BECAUSE HE IS THE SINNER'S FRIEND
BECAUSE HE CONQUERED DEATH AND SIN
BECAUSE HE SPEAKS TO THE DEEPEST NEEDS OF
    MY HEART
BECAUSE HE IS INFINITELY PATIENT WITH ME
BECAUSE HE IS RETURNING TO TAKE ME TO
    HIMSELF
BECAUSE HE HATES EVIL
BECAUSE HE ALONE WAS CRUCIFIED FOR
    WRETCHED SINNERS
BECAUSE HE IS THE BAD PERSON'S GOD
BECAUSE HE IS PREPARING A PLACE FOR ME
BECAUSE HE LOVES THE UNLOVABLE
BECAUSE HE OVERCOMES THE DARKNESS
BECAUSE HE REJOICES OVER ME
BECAUSE HIS DESIRE IS FOR ME
BECAUSE HE RULES OVER HISTORY
BECAUSE HE DESIRES A FULL HEAVEN
BECAUSE HE WILL JUDGE THE NATIONS
BECAUSE HE TOUCHED THE LEPER
BECAUSE HE MADE THE DEAF TO HEAR

BECAUSE HE RAISED LAZARUS
BECAUSE HE IS LIKE RAIN ON A MOWN FIELD
BECAUSE HE REVEALS HIMSELF TO MUSLIMS IN
    DREAMS
BECAUSE HE IS FAIRER THAN TEN THOUSAND
BECAUSE HE WALKED ON WATER
BECAUSE HE IS NOT RELIGIOUS
BECAUSE HE WILL SHAKE THE NATIONS
BECAUSE HE REIGNS BY THE POWER OF AN
    INDESTRUCTIBLE LIFE
BECAUSE IN HIM ARE ALL THE TREASURES OF
    WISDOM AND KNOWLEDGE
BECAUSE HE HAS GOOD PLANS FOR ME
BECAUSE HE IS ABLE TO PRESENT ME FAULTLESS
    BEFORE HIS FATHER'S THRONE WITH GREAT
    JOY